Wild Bill Hickok

TAMES THE WEST

WILD BILL HICKOK

TAMES THE WEST

───────── ★ ─────────

by STEWART H. HOLBROOK

Illustrated by ERNEST RICHARDSON

RANDOM HOUSE · NEW YORK

To the Reader

THE CAREER OF WILD BILL HICKOK WAS SO filled with violence that his genuine contribution to the West has been all but lost in the din of many battles and the clouds of powder-blue smoke.

To see him in his proper place we must keep in mind a few simple facts: He never killed but in self-defense or in line of duty; he never sought trouble; and to the lawless elements of the old frontier he represented their worst enemy, which was Law and Order.

Hence, Hickok was a marked man, always on the spot, a man who had to be just a little quicker than any of the ugly and mostly worthless characters he found it necessary to shoot in the process of civilizing the West.

Wild Bill Hickok was the man, more than any other, who tamed and quieted the border settlements from the time they were founded until the day when official law arrived at last and could take over the task of making life secure and property safe. He performed his great pioneer work single-handed and with rigid honesty and supreme courage. Little wonder the West continues to honor the memory of its incomparable peace officer, who was *the* landmark of order in the midst of turbulence and crime.

STEWART HOLBROOK

Contents

1. A BOY ON THE FRONTIER 3
2. TROUBLE ON THE CANAL 13
3. WEST TO BLOODY KANSAS 21
4. ON THE SANTA FE TRAIL 34
5. HICKOK HAS TO KILL 41
6. HICKOK BECOMES WILD BILL . . . 51
7. HICKOK, THE UNION SPY 67
8. SCOUTING FOR CUSTER 78
9. TAMING A WILD TOWN 95
10. ABILENE WAS TOUGH 108
11. A ROUNDUP TRAGEDY 122
12. A NIGHT IN DODGE CITY 133
13. SHOW BUSINESS 141
14. THE BLACK HILLS 154
15. . . . WITH HIS BOOTS ON 165

Full-page illustrations

"I want to get to Kansas," Hickok told the mate 27

"Go on home, boys," he called out . . . 55

Wild Bill's knife was out 91

"Clear out!" called the city marshal . . 119

Wild Bill drew a gun and shot the lamp to splinters! 151

McCall drew his gun, stepped close behind Hickok 173

Wild Bill Hickok

TAMES THE WEST

1: A Boy on the Frontier

AT LAST CAME A MOONLESS NIGHT. HERE AND
there a candle or lamp struggled feebly from a
window but made no impression on the darkness
that covered the settlement of Troy Grove on the
Illinois frontier.

It was the kind of night Alonzo W. Hickok had
been waiting for. He called two of his four sons.

"Horace," said he, "you and James go hitch the team. No loud talking. Do it quietly."

The two boys slipped out of the Green Mountain House, their father's small hotel, and like shadows moved to the barn. Horace was thirteen. James was ten. James was the Hickok son who was to become famous as Wild Bill.

With little more than a few whispers the two lads harnessed a pair of fine black horses, and hitched them to a long farm wagon. Then they stood, horses and boys, in the barnyard, waiting. Even the animals seemed to sense the need for quiet. The only sound in all that immense darkness came from the nearby woods, where an owl called mournfully.

Inside the house Polly Hickok, the boys' mother, was working swiftly in the kitchen. She wrapped two great loaves of bread in a newspaper. In another package she put generous slices of cooked venison, several sour pickles, and a small paper of salt. Into a bag went a dozen apples. "It's ready," she said to her husband.

Alonzo Hickok opened a trapdoor in the kitchen floor that led into the darkness of the cellar. He held a candle close to the opening. "Come, my friends," he called softly, and up the ladder out of the gloom climbed four Negroes—three young men and an old woman.

The dark faces shone in the dim light. There was no fear in their eyes, yet these runaway slaves from the South understood the dangers of their situation. They were passengers on the Underground Railroad.

There were of course no rails on the Underground. It was merely the name applied to several secret routes over which escaped slaves from the Southern states fled north and eventually into Canada. In that country they found safety against capture and return to their masters.

Hickok's Green Mountain House at Troy Grove was one of the many stations on the Underground. Alonzo Hickok, a native of anti-slavery Vermont, had risked his life again and again in aiding Negroes in their flights to freedom.

For nearly a week the three young men and the old woman had been hiding in the Hickok cellar, while Mr. Hickok prayed and waited for a suitable night. This was it. Now he could move his four charges with less danger to the next station on the Underground. This was at a settlement called Panton's Mills, some thirty miles from Troy Grove.

Mrs. Hickok gave the packages of food to the Negroes.

"Follow me," said Mr. Hickok. His wife doused the candle. The door opened softly. Out of the house went Hickok and the fugitives, who were motioned to get into the wagon body.

Horace and James Hickok covered the Negroes with sacks and old quilts; then both boys got into the driver's seat beside their father, who took the reins. He gave the reins a slight tug. The horses moved forward. The wheels of the Underground Railroad had again begun to turn.

It was intensely dark. The night seemed to bear down as though it had weight, like a heavy wool blanket. Not a glimmer of candle showed in the silent village. Even so, it was only after they had cleared the last house of the sleeping hamlet that Mr. Hickok touched the horses lightly with the whip. They responded at once, going into a jog trot.

Nobody spoke, least of all ten-year-old James Hickok. This was the first time he had been allowed to make a trip on the Underground. He was elated with the mystery and the danger of it. It was a night, he said much later, that he never forgot.

For perhaps ten miles or so the party moved on without incident through the night. Then, the unusually sharp eyes of young James Hickok caught something the others did not see.

"Dad," he said, "there is somebody, or something, beside the road, up ahead."

"I don't see anything, son."

"It's there, but I can't tell what it is. It moved."

"We'll soon find out." The elder Hickok

reached into the wagon back of the seat and picked up the sawed-off smoothbore that he called his shotgun. He placed it between his legs. "Get on, get on," he called to the horses.

A moment later the Hickoks saw not one but two figures emerge from the dark and approach the road. Mr. Hickok pulled up the team and they slowed to a stop.

"What do you want?" Mr. Hickok asked.

"What you got in the wagon?" one of the strangers countered.

"Who wants to know?"

"We do. Looking for some nigras might come along here."

Both strangers came closer to the wagon. There was a tense moment. Young James Hickok began to feel sweat on his forehead. His mouth felt dry. Then his father spoke.

"I haven't seen any Negroes," he said, and then he suddenly slapped the horses. They snorted with surprise, then leaped into a dead run.

"Stop! Stop! Hold on!" the two strangers were shouting.

On went the wagon bounding on the rough road.

"Down, boys, down!" commanded Mr. Hickok. The boys crouched low in the wagon seat.

Just then a flash came out of the dark, and a bullet whined over the heads of the boys. The frightened horses leaped faster. Another blast came from the rear, and again James Hickok heard the mean singing overhead.

"Horace, take the reins," and Mr. Hickok passed them to the older boy, turned around on the seat, and brought his gun to his shoulder. He fired into the air, toward the rear, not trying to aim.

"That'll let them know we have a gun," he said, and reloaded.

Perhaps the return fire did give the slave-catchers pause. Something did, anyway, for there seemed to be no pursuit.

After a mile of running, the team slowed to a walk. Horace was still driving, while Mr. Hickok and James sat at the tail of the wagon body, watching for any sign of a chase.

Mr. Hickok comforted the Negroes hidden beneath the sacks. "Don't be afraid. We are in the clear now."

To James Hickok the miles seemed to pass with a terrible slowness. After what seemed many hours, he noticed that he could see trees, and distinguish a field here and there. And once, far off, he heard the morning call of a rooster.

Dawn was breaking when the Hickok party drove into the yard of a modest frame house on the edge of Panton's Mills. James was sent to rap. When a tall man, very sleepy, opened the door, the boy spoke up.

"Mr. Henry, we are the Hickoks. We have some people for you."

The tall man woke up immediately. "Yes, my lad," he said, "I was expecting you last night."

"Father didn't think it was a good time then."

"Go fetch him, son. Bring in your party. No time to lose. It will be light soon."

The four fugitives came out of the wagon. "Praise God Almighty!" exclaimed the old woman. "Praise God and His Underground Railroad!"

They went into the Henry house. They were one station more on the way to freedom. The Henrys would move them again, come night.

The Hickoks went into the house, too, and Mrs. Henry set out tea and bread, while Mr. Hickok related the brush they had had with the two slave-catchers.

"I know they are slave-catchers," he said. "We had seen them around Troy Grove for a few days. Pretended to be looking for sheep and cattle to buy."

"Yes," said Mr. Henry, "we heard here there were two catchers in the neighborhood. But we never saw any suspicious characters."

"If I were you," said Mr. Hickok, "I don't

think I'd try to move these people again until you are certain the coast is clear."

"I shan't. We haven't got a cellar here, but the Negroes can stay in the hay-mow in the barn."

"You will find them quiet enough. They know things are pretty hot all the way north to Galena."

There was some small talk, then the Hickoks prepared to return home. The old colored woman came to thank them, which she did with a grace and dignity which James Hickok remembered all his life. "Bless you all!" she said, weeping with emotion. "Bless you one and all." She made young James think he had done something wonderful. He felt good all over.

These four were neither the first nor the last slaves that the Hickok family helped on their way to liberty. But this was the first time that James, later Wild Bill, had been under fire, the first time he had heard the whistle and zing of bullets close by. In the next twenty-nine years he was to hear more than his share of such music.

2: Trouble on the Canal

IT WAS NATURAL THAT THE HICKOK BOYS
learned the use of firearms at an early age. Guns
were part of life on the frontier; they meant food
and clothing.

By the time he was twelve, James was a re-
markably good shot, better than his older
brother. He trapped and hunted along Little

13

Vermillion River near the Hickok home, getting meat for the family table, and furs for caps and also for sale. For twenty muskrat pelts and the skins of half a dozen mink, he became owner of a fine rifle. He now suggested to his parents that he devote all his time to hunting.

Mr. and Mrs. Hickok, however, had other plans. They were determined that all their children should have such education as the pioneer settlement offered.

The school at Troy Grove was very good for a frontier village. There, much against his wishes, young James learned to read and write, to "do sums," as arithmetic was called, to study geography, and also to read American history.

Yet at every opportunity, James took his fine new rifle and ranged the woods. His marksmanship improved steadily. By the time he was fourteen, he was rated a better shot than most of the grown men in the neighborhood.

But tragedy was near. In 1852, the elder Hickok died, leaving six children but little money. The boys would have to find steady work.

Fifteen-year-old James, who had always been very good with horses, got a job driving freighting teams for a local merchant. This really was man's work, and Jim Hickok believed he was a man, in spite of his years. The freighting work went on for many months. The trouble with it was that it wasn't steady enough. James would make a trip that occupied perhaps two weeks. This might be followed by a period of two weeks, or longer, when there was nothing to do.

James was looking for something else when a large gang of men moved into the county to dig a section of a canal. The wages paid for this work were much higher than those paid by local merchants or other employers.

By this time Jim Hickok was seventeen. He was a tall, well-built youth, alert and quick of movement. The foreman of the canal crew was glad to hire him as a common laborer. The young man soon showed he was a willing worker, able to hold his own with ax or spade.

A good many of the canal laborers were foot-loose wanderers, and among them were several very tough men. Drinking and fighting were their chief entertainment. One of these hoboes was a bad actor named Hudson, a teamster. He was to bring about a sudden change in young Hickok's life.

Teamster Hudson was a large man with a terrible temper. He was cruel to his horses, and mean to his helpers, especially if they were boys or smaller men than he. Half a dozen helpers had quit the canal rather than work with Hudson. Perhaps that is what gave the canal gang boss an idea.

"Jim Hickok," the boss said one day, "you start tomorrow as Hudson's helper. You will get two bits more a day for wages."

"Yes, sir," Jim said, but he was anything but pleased. He had never in his life been in a fight.

He knew Hudson's bullying ways. Other young men had told him that Hudson used his whip not only on his team but on his helpers too.

For several days all went well. Then Hudson started to find fault. Everything Jim did was wrong. Hudson yelled at him, and snarled and roared. One day he called young Hickok a vile name.

Jim dropped the chain he was about to hitch to a log. He walked over to Hudson. His face was white, his knees shaking. His voice choked as he spoke.

"That isn't my name."

"Ho, ho—so that isn't your name?" Hudson jeered. "Well, young squirt, that's the name I'll give you from now on."

Jim Hickok said not a word. Instead, he leaped at the big man. Hudson fell back, dropping his reins. Hickok was at him again. This time they grappled.

"Fight, fight!" the shout went up, and mem-

bers of the crew came running over to the edge of the canal where the battle was on. No one attempted to interfere.

Hickok broke away from Hudson, stepped back, then drove his right fist into the man's face. Blood flowed. With a roar Hudson reached for the boy again. Hickok dodged, then struck Hudson again—hard. The man reeled. Hickok was at him, punching, punching. He was in a fury, and the bystanders yelled with joy to watch him beat the older and bigger man.

Hudson clinched. Both went down. A moment later they rolled off the bank and splashed into the canal. Down they went out of sight.

Hickok came up and was quickly pulled to land. A hundred men were swarming around. Jim Hickok spat water from his mouth. He was not injured, but he was frightened. What if Hudson had been drowned? What if the man were now lying on the bottom of the deep ditch? While all eyes were on the water, watching for Hudson's head to appear, Jim Hickok, certain now that he was an unintentional murderer, ran into the nearby woods.

The lad was out of sight and out of sound when Hudson at last came to the surface. He was helped to shore, a completely subdued man, jeered at by his fellows for having been beaten by a boy.

But Jim Hickok did not know this. It was more than a year before he did know it. But now, here in the dark of the timber, he sat down to think. What was he to do?

His fears mounted. He could hear a faint shouting from the direction of the canal. Probably they were pulling Hudson's dead body from the water. Yes, that was it. They would soon be looking for the murderer, too. Might get bloodhounds from LaSalle. Anyhow, the sheriff and a posse would be out looking, beating the bush, looking for him, Jim Hickok.

Yes, and then there would be the jail. After the jail, there would be a hanging. That's what they did with murderers. They hanged them by the neck until they were dead. The judge always said that. Jim had heard about it. Until you were dead . . .

But they wouldn't catch Jim Hickok. No, sir. Not here, in the woods. He would go away, and if they caught him at all, it would be far off. Perhaps out West.

When darkness fell, Jim Hickok, lonely and still frightened, worked his way westward, heading toward what he hoped would be the Mississippi River.

3: West to Bloody Kansas

FOUR DAYS AFTER THE BATTLE AT THE CANAL, Jim Hickok at last reached a boat landing on the great Mississippi. It was merely a wood-stop, where the stern-wheelers stocked up with fuel. Near this wharf, piled cordwood covered many acres.

On his way overland, Jim had picked up a

piece of useful information: you could get a free ride on the Mississippi river boats if you'd help the crew to load the slabwood. Jim walked along the wharf, looking for whoever was boss. The boss turned out to be a fellow almost seven feet tall and, in the style of frontier humor, was thus known as Stub.

As Jim spoke to the man, a handsome great boat was approaching, and she blew for the landing.

"Sure, young feller," Stub replied. "You're just in time. Get busy passing that there wood as soon as this stern-wheeler docks. They'll give you a free ride to St. Louis. Feed you good, too."

The boat came to dock with a great ringing of bells and backing water. Roustabouts appeared to catch the hawsers and make her fast. A troop of wood-passers came down the gangplank.

"Here, young feller," Stub shouted. "Here's your gang. Get a move on." Hickok watched a moment, then picked up a couple of heavy long slabs and carried them to the boat's side. Here they were tossed down a chute.

Less than half an hour later, the boat cast off, sounded her whistle, and moved briskly out into mid-stream. Jim Hickok was there on the fore-deck watching the land slide by. It was the first time he had ever been on the water in anything bigger than a rowboat.

Jim leaned on a capstan and watched Illinois slide past. He was on his own now. He rather liked it, too, even if he had no idea what he would do in St. Louis.

It was wonderful, this life on the great river he had heard so much about. Big boats and lit-tle boats, they were going by in what seemed like a parade. In their bright paint and with their graceful lines they made real pictures. Towns and what appeared like big cities to young Hickok could be seen every few miles. He almost forgot he was running away from what he thought surely was a charge of murder.

His luck still held good on the big levee at

St. Louis. A man in uniform asked him to help
unload freight carried on the same ship which
had taken him to this teeming place where hundreds of men, both white and colored, labored
day and night. For a few hours of work, the
man gave him a big silver dollar. You would
think money here grew like potatoes back home!

In a boarding house near the docks, where
Jim got lodging for the night, all the talk was of
Kansas. Seemed as if almost everybody was try-
ing to get to Kansas.

What made Kansas such an exciting place was
that it had become a battleground for the pro-
slavery and the anti-slavery forces. Young Hickok
heard a man say that a law had been passed
to let Kansas Territory enter the Union as either
a state where slavery was permitted, or banned.
It was up to the voters of the Territory.

St. Louis and other cities of the South or near-
South were swarming with politicians who were
determined Kansas should be a slave state. They

were encouraging thousands of Southern people to move into the Territory, stake claims to farm lands, and to form a local government free of Northern sympathizers.

"If I was a bit younger," said the man in the lodging house, "I'd sure head for Kansas. Going to be wild times there, no fooling. And I'd like nothing better than to drive the Yankees out of there."

Young Hickok put in a word. "Mister," he asked, "haven't Yankees any rights in Kansas? I mean, can't they live there?"

"They wouldn't live there if I could help it."

"But is there a law against their going to Kansas?" Jim wanted to know.

"No. There ain't no law. But I tell you, young feller, there's a heap of good Southern folks heading for there and when they get there, the Yanks will have to leave."

Jim Hickok said nothing. He had already made up his mind to see Kansas. He remembered the many slaves he had seen, running away, risking their lives, anything to escape their masters. Yes, he would go to Kansas.

He got his chance first thing next morning. Docked at the levee was the steamer *Imperial*, a fine-looking boat. She was about to leave. A sign at her gangplank indicated she was going up the Missouri River to Kansas City, then to a place named Leavenworth, Kansas.

This was the boat he wanted. In no time at all, for he now had more assurance, Hickok had found and approached the *Imperial's* mate. "I want to get to Kansas," he told that worthy.

"Well, m'lad, this is the right boat."

"But I haven't any money."

The mate looked at Hickok and saw a rugged tall youth.

"Can you load wood?"

"You bet I can," Jim replied. "I loaded wood all the way down from some place near Quincy."

"Come, get aboard. We have plenty of fuel now. You'll get a chance to work later. I'll give

"I want to get to Kansas," Hickok told the mate.

you free meals, a good bunk, and a dollar if you stay with us as far as Leavenworth."

Ten minutes later the *Imperial* sounded her whistle, and Jim Hickok, a man of the world, was on his way to Kansas—Bloody Kansas, he heard someone call it.

The new settlement of Leavenworth, Kansas, turned out to be a madhouse of activity. It seemed even busier than had St. Louis or Kansas City. Steamers were coming and leaving, their whistles adding to the din of dock workers and the shouts of several hundred teamsters getting under way with huge wagon trains, heading for towns back from the river.

Stretched out for a mile from the wharf was a muddy street banked by board shacks that were mostly saloons and dance halls. Bedlam welled out of these places. Drunken men lurched up and down in the mud. And as far as the eye could reach were the wagon trains—hundreds of wagons, thousands of mules and horses. They went on and on over the horizon.

It was Jim Hickok's first sight of the new Wild West. Illinois was a back number now, a settled and civilized place compared to this raw country. The frontier had moved west hundreds of miles within a short year or so. This was the rambunctious region on which this young man was to have so much influence. He could hardly have guessed it, as he stood there at the teeming collection of huts on the prairie.

Jim Hickok did not tarry in the settlement of Leavenworth. He hired out to work for a farmer two miles out. His first job was breaking the tough virgin soil with a huge plow and six horses. He liked it.

At this period, and for reasons never known, Jim Hickok began calling himself Bill. Perhaps the youngster thought the change of name would throw any possible pursuers off his trail. It wouldn't, of course, but maybe he thought it would. So he was now Bill Hickok. The other part of his famous name was to come a little later.

Bill Hickok developed a restlessness and within a few months he moved to Johnson County. It was there he started to learn some of the many things that would stand him in good stead later.

He first hired out to work for John W. Owens, a white man who had married a Shawnee squaw. Bill liked the Owens family, who had several children, and they came to think the world of him. He let his bright yellow hair grow long, the way the Indians did. He never had it cut short again.

At the Owens' place Bill began to learn to speak Shawnee. He was fascinated with Indian customs and lore. Few white men paid the Indians much attention, save to rob them. Bill Hickok learned readily everything they would teach him, including their cures for sicknesses, the preparation of Indian foods, the making of garments and their various beliefs.

How useful these things would later become to Hickok he could have had no idea.

Meanwhile, the struggle for Kansas was going on. Old John Brown and his sons had come among the immigrants from the North. They had been preaching and committing violence. So had countless adventurers from Missouri and Tennessee.

The struggle between the Free-Staters and the Slave-Staters had begun and blood had flowed here and there. The nights had been lighted from the flames of burning barns and houses. There would be more trouble before the whole United States at last erupted in Civil War.

The Northerners in Kansas organized a Free-State army and called for recruits. John Owens and Bill Hickok signed up. Both were in the fighting at Bull Creek, when the Free-Staters met and defeated the slavery forces.

Hickok and Owens also took part in the dangerous job of getting a shipment of several hundred Sharps rifles out of St. Louis and to the Free-State town of Lawrence, Kansas. There the weapons were distributed. They were of the greatest importance in driving the pro-slavery elements from the region. As a result, Kansas was brought into the Union on the side of the North.

This was all good training for the young man who was to help civilize Kansas.

Remington Cal. 44
Army Revolver Pat. 1858

4: On the Santa Fe Trail

SOME NOTION OF WHAT HIS PLACE ON THE
frontier was going to be might well have come
to young Bill Hickok in 1858. In that year, when
he had just turned twenty-one, the settlers of
Monticello, Kansas, elected him constable. As
the only police officer in the township, he proved

able and bold. Monticello was soon known for an orderliness which was unusual in a region that was still wild and woolly.

The Reed Hotel in Monticello was a stop on the stage route between the settlements of eastern Kansas and Topeka. Bill Hickok, always a good hand with horses, was put in charge of the hotel stable. When a driver was sick, or merely drunk, which was often, Bill took his place, driving stages to Lawrence, Leavenworth, Topeka, and other towns on the route. He discovered that he liked the life of a stage driver.

So, in the summer of 1859, Bill quit his job in Monticello and moved west. A month later, at Independence, Missouri, he climbed aboard a big coach pulled by six mules, and started his first trip over the famous trail that led to Santa Fe, New Mexico.

The Santa Fe trail also led over the Rocky Mountains. This was far different from driving stage on the level prairie. The road was at best rough. It often ran at a dizzying height on rock shelves high above canyons, with barely room to get around the curves.

Bill Hickok was a master; he drove with the greatest care but with a flourish that Westerners admired. And he always brought the coach into Santa Fe on the dead run, making a heap of noise and raising much dust. To see him ending a trip was soon one of the sights in Santa Fe.

Here in the old town at the end of the Trail young Bill Hickok met one of the greatest characters of the American West. This was Kit Carson, the famous scout. They spent much time together between Bill's runs, and ever afterward Bill Hickok enjoyed telling of his acquaintance with the great Kit Carson.

Meanwhile, Hickok had displayed such ability on the Trail that the company picked him to take charge of a huge caravan of freight wagons on a trip over the difficult Raton Mountains. Hickok met the wagon train near Bent's Fort. He spaced the wagons widely apart, and escorted each one separately over the worst places of the trail. Not a wagon was lost, or even in difficulty. Yet, right after accomplishing this feat, Bill nearly lost his life.

It happened when he was heading back to Kansas on horseback. While he was still high in the mountains, his animal snorted in fright and suddenly leaped sideways. Just then a tremendous grizzly bear plunged out of the bushes and started for him. As Bill fell from his horse, one of his revolvers dropped from its holster. Before he could retrieve it, the bear was upon him.

Pulling his other gun, Bill fired six times at close range, hitting the huge animal with every shot. The bullets might as well have been grains of rice. The great beast came on without pause. There was only one thing left: Bill drew his long knife from its sheath. Just then the bear struck him with one paw, ripping Bill's shirt and the flesh of his left shoulder into ribbons.

Bill sunk the bowie knife into the animal's side. He drew it out, then plunged it again. He struck the bear in the neck and sides, and

twice in the belly. The crazed beast now tried
to get at the man, to hug him. Bill realized
what a hug would mean. But he knew he must
stay close to the animal. That was his only
chance to kill her.

But for all his youth and strength, Bill Hickok
began to tire. He was pawed and cut all over,
bleeding profusely. In trying to dodge a new
rush, his foot caught on a stone. The snarling
animal closed in, frothing horribly. This seemed

to be the end. In one last effort, Bill struck the bear again with all his might, and as the long blade sank into the flesh, he felt the animal suddenly loosen her hold.

Bill struck again and again, as hot blood poured out of the bear's wounds in a flood. The beast was sorely hurt, but she was still alive. She reached out a paw and caught Bill on top of his head with a terrible swipe. The flesh gave way and Bill was blinded as his own scalp fell down over his eyes. He felt his legs weaken. He slumped, then fell to the ground. The last thing he was conscious of was feeling his left arm in the hot jaws of the bear.

An hour or so later, along the trail came a freight wagon, heading for Santa Fe, and its driver never forgot the scene in the road. He saw a huge bear, motionless, partly lying on a man who did not move. The man's left arm was in the bear's mouth.

The driver recognized Bill Hickok at once, and thought he was as dead as the bear. Bill's scalp was hanging down over his face. His chest, his arms, thighs and legs, all were horribly torn. He was bleeding from a score of wounds. But he still breathed.

The driver got Bill out from under the bear. He patched him up as best he could, laid him in the wagon, and took him to Santa Fe. That he lived and made a full recovery, except for scars that remained during his lifetime, was accounted one of the wonders of the Santa Fe Trail.

5: Hickok Has to Kill

YOUNG BILL HICKOK, AGED TWENTY-TWO, was standing the toughening process of the West in pretty good shape. His abilities were also appreciated. To aid his recovery from the battle with the bear, the stage company sent him to Rock Creek Station on the Oregon Trail, where his duties would be light.

Rock Creek Station was considered one of the quietest spots in the West, the right place for a man to heal his wounds and regain his strength.

That was what the stage company thought. But Rock Creek Station turned out to be anything but quiet for Bill Hickok.

In charge of the station was a somewhat notorious character named Dave McCanles who had fled West after getting into some sort of trouble while acting as sheriff in North Carolina.

McCanles was a hard-working and aggressive man who, in addition to his job with the stage company, operated a ranch of his own. He was a born leader, and Hickok soon discovered that McCanles had surrounded himself with a crew of reckless followers. Several of these were of the most doubtful character. They were always coming and going, and what they did elsewhere seemed to be a secret. There were usually from six to ten of them living at the station or at the McCanles ranch nearby.

McCanles put Hickok to work in the stables. His left arm was still in a sling, and he was still weak from the terrible beating he had taken from the grizzly.

Whatever the cause, Dave McCanles took an immediate dislike to Bill Hickok. When his gang was around, McCanles enjoyed grabbing Bill and throwing him to the ground. This was hardly playful, considering the mending arm.

But Bill couldn't do much about it. Simply moving his arm gave him great pain. So, he made the best of it and pretended, as McCanles did, that it was all in fun.

Within a few weeks of Bill's arrival, McCanles sold his interest in Rock Creek Station to the Overland Stage Company, which put Horace Wellman in charge. McCanles continued to live on his ranch near the station.

Through some oversight in the main office of the Overland Company, payment to McCanles for sale of the station did not come immediately.

McCanles began to demand the money of Agent Wellman, who had no authority to settle Mc-Canles' claims.

McCanles turned to threats. He ordered Well-man to turn the station and all the company property over to him, and then to get out. Well-man quite properly refused.

McCanles returned to his ranch and called several of his gang together. "Boys," he told them, "I can't get my rightful money from this Wellman feller. I ordered him and his wife to get out. They told me they were staying."

"Well," said Jim Woods, a sort of lieutenant to McCanles, "are we going to let them stay?"

"No, we are not," McCanles insisted. "I aim to clean out the place."

"Bill Hickok is there," Woods told his boss. "You know that?"

"Yes, I know it. I'm going to run him off, too, if he so much as opens his mouth."

"He ain't even well yet," said Woods.

"Makes no difference," McCanles replied. "He goes too."

Jim Gordon, another of the gang, spoke up: "Why don't we go over there now? It's getting tame around here."

"Let's have a bite to eat first," McCanles said. "Let's eat, then we'll go to Rock Creek and see who owns that place, anyhow. I'm tired of waiting."

After a quick bite, McCanles strapped on his belt that held two revolvers. Jim Woods and Jim Gordon armed themselves. So did McCanles' son, Monroe. The four men mounted and rode the short distance to the station.

"You fellers stay here," McCanles told his men as they came up to the station barn. "I'll go up to the house. You can see everything that goes on from here. Come on the run if need be."

"Dad, I'm going with you." It was young Mc-Canles.

"Come on, then."

The two men tied their horses. They walked quickly up to the west end of the house. Wellman heard them coming. He came out into the dooryard.

Dave McCanles opened up with a perfect tirade of abuse, calling Wellman all sorts of names. Wellman tried to break in to protest. McCanles raged on.

"Get your woman and then get out of here," he shouted. "And I mean now!" The man seemed more than half crazed with his anger. Wellman, afraid for his life, turned and went into the house.

The fiery Mrs. Wellman now came out. "McCanles," she cried, "I defy you to turn us out. We . . . "

"Go way," yelled McCanles. "I ain't dealing with no women. I got business with your husband."

McCanles raved on.

At that instant somebody else came into the picture. Bill Hickok came out the door. He pushed Mrs. Wellman to one side, then he stepped in front, facing McCanles and his son.

Bill didn't say anything. There he stood, a tall, lithe figure, eyes half closed but the slits revealing what looked like bits of blue ice.

McCanles suddenly stopped his raving. He had forgotten about Hickok. The sight sobered him, too, even though Bill's left arm was still in a sling.

McCanles started to parley. Bill spoke not a word. McCanles was obviously troubled as to what to do next.

"You and me, we're friends, ain't we?" he asked. "Ain't we, Hickok?"

"I guess so," Bill replied. It wasn't an enthusiastic reply.

"Then send Wellman out here. I want to settle with him. If you don't send him out, I'll have to go in and drag him out."

Hickok looked intently at McCanles for a long minute. McCanles felt uneasy under the cold stare of this tall young man. Then, without saying a word, Hickok turned and went back into the house.

McCanles and his son thereupon left the west door and walked around to the front door, on the south side. From here McCanles could see the interior of the entire house, except for a small alcove screened by a calico curtain. He wanted to know what was going on inside.

Wellman and Hickok were in the big room. But McCanles did not enter. He was still trying to figure out what to do next. Hickok's presence had made him wary.

What McCanles finally did was to ask for a drink of water. Hickok came forward. He dipped a gourd of water from a pail on the table. This he handed to McCanles.

As McCanles lifted the gourd to drink, Hickok moved quickly behind the calico curtain.

McCanles sensed his danger. "Come out of there," he called. "Come out or I'll come get you."

"When you try that, there will be one less skunk around here." It was Hickok.

McCanles drew a gun. He took a step into the house. Hickok fired. The bullet went through McCanles' heart. He staggered back and fell to the ground beside the doorsill.

Down at the stable McCanles' men heard the shot. The two of them came forward on the run, drawing as they ran. Jim Woods ran for the west door, Jim Gordon for the south door, where lay the body of his boss.

What Mr. and Mrs. Wellman were doing isn't clear. They were not needed, anyway.

Just as Woods, gun in hand, entered the west door, Hickok shot him dead.

A moment later Gordon arrived at the south door. He saw Woods fall, and he turned to run. It was too late. Hickok stepped clear of the smoke swirling around in the house, and then fired. Gordon was hit, but he ran on toward his horse.

Hickok now stepped out of the house and shot the fleeing man again. That was the end of Gordon. It was also the end of the battle.

Young Monroe McCanles made no effort to get into the fight. He was told to return to the McCanles ranch.

Bill Hickok remained at Rock Creek station, having sent Horace Wellman to Beatrice (now in Nebraska) to notify the sheriff that Hickok had killed three men. Hickok's arrest took place a few days later. He was tried at Beatrice, and a jury found him not guilty. His plea was self-defense.

The verdict proved a popular one, for public sentiment was almost wholly with Hickok.

But the affray was for many years a controversial subject in the West. McCanles had many friends. So did Hickok. For the next forty years, or as long as any of them lived, they argued the merits of the Rock Creek battle.

6: *Hickok Becomes Wild Bill*

WHEN BILL HICKOK WAS FREED BY THE court at Beatrice, the time was July of 1861. The great struggle between North and South had begun. The Civil War had been going on for two months.

There had never been any doubt in Bill Hickok's mind as to which side he was on. He had never forgotten those pitiful black refugees on

51

the Underground Railroad. Now that he had been cleared of guilt in the affair at Rock Creek Station, he mounted a horse and rode to Fort Leavenworth, Kansas. There he offered his services to the government officers.

Hickok's abilities were well known in Leavenworth. He was immediately asked to take charge of a wagon train of supplies going to Union troops in Missouri.

Though the train was a big one, only twelve soldiers were detailed as guards. That was scarcely sufficient. On the third day out of Fort Leavenworth, the train was attacked by Confederate guerrillas, fifty strong, all mounted and well armed. The train was captured. But not Hickok. When called upon to surrender, he spurred his horse and rode off under heavy rifle fire.

Hickok rode at high speed to Independence, Missouri, which was garrisoned by Union troops, and reported the loss of the train to the commanding officer. He was told that no help was available. He must ride on to Kansas City.

Bill's horse was tired. So was Bill. Both must have some rest for the hard trip to Kansas City. Bill stabled his animal, then set out to find a place where he could sleep for a few hours.

Independence was crowded, and excited. War was at her very doors. The town was running over with refugees from the surrounding region who were seeking safety. Added to these were gangs of rowdies and cutthroats, bent on violence and easy pickings. Local police seemed unable to do anything about them.

While walking down one of the main streets, Bill came to a mob of rough-looking characters who had surrounded a small house. Roaring drunk, they were waving guns, shooting into the air, and shouting.

Bill stopped on the edge of the crowd. He learned the drunks were planning to lynch a man accused of wounding a teamster in an argument. The man had fled into the small house, and there he was awaiting what must have seemed like certain death.

"Where's the constable?" Bill asked of a sober man.

"Constable?" jeered the fellow. "He's probably hiding somewhere. This crowd's mean drunk."

"So they seem," Hickok said. He wormed his way forward through the howling mob. When he got close to the house, he drew both of his guns. He jumped up on top of a low fence, and there he stood, a Colt in each hand, waving for attention.

"Go on home, boys," he called out. "Go home, or there will be trouble here."

The crowd started to mutter. A few men made motions with drawn bowie knives. Hickok waved his guns again but did not shoot. And he called out again: "Go home! If you don't, there will be more dead men around here in the next five minutes than this town can bury in a week."

You can't tell about drunks. They are queer. You never know how anything will strike them. What Hickok was doing, besides risking his life,

"Go on home, boys," he called out.

was taking a chance that he could talk these drunks into going away and forgetting about their intended victim.

Hickok had judged well. He had scarcely shouted his preposterous threat when a few of the drunken rowdies began to cheer him. And then, in the officious manner of drunks wanting to be useful, they joined Bill in his demand that the crowd disperse. "Go home, boys. Go home," they chanted, pushing and urging as if they were peace officers bent on doing their duty.

By this time, a tanned old veteran of the Santa Fe trail had recognized Hickok as the famous stage driver. He came forward to shake Bill's hand and to praise him for holding the mob at bay. Bill thanked him, and went on asking the drunks to move on. In a few minutes they had scattered elsewhere up and down the street.

Now Hickok called to the poor fellow hiding in the house. "You better go somewhere else for tonight," he said. "Some of these drunks might remember what they started out to do and come back." Then Bill resumed his search for a quiet place to sleep.

As Hickok swung back into the main street, the old Santa Fe veteran and a dozen more characters who remembered Bill from days on the plains surrounded him. They lifted him up on their shoulders, then paraded up the street, cheering, to the public square. Here within a few minutes at least a thousand persons congregated, wondering what was going on.

The whole affair had turned into a demonstration for the tall young man who had stopped the murderous mob. In the crowd were many women. One of these—and neither Bill nor anyone else ever learned who she was—stepped forward and gave him the name he was to wear until his death.

"Good for you, Wild Bill!" That was what the unknown woman shouted in a clear high voice.

It isn't known why a simple thing like that will take the public's fancy. Such things cannot be planned. They must just happen, and they must somehow stir the imagination.

"Good for you, Wild Bill!" the woman had cried. And it was enough. From that moment, he who had been born James Butler Hickok, was Wild Bill.

As for Wild Bill, he wound up that night sleeping in the stable with his horse.

Early next morning he was riding for Kansas City. From the Union commandant there he secured a troop of a hundred hard-riding cavalrymen.

Riding at the head of this troop, Hickok led them to the scene of the attack on his wagon train. A few miles beyond this place they caught up with the fifty-odd Confederate guerrillas, and attacked at once, scattering them and recapturing the mules, wagons, and most of the supplies. Bill then had the train re-form and with his troopers accompanied it safely to Independence.

Wild Bill had completed his first assignment

of the war. He now went to the Union commander in Missouri and asked what else he could do. Missouri was becoming more turbulent by the day. It contained many Northern sympathizers, and an even larger number of pro-slavery people. Both sides were determined to drive the other out of the state.

Wild Bill's reputation was already known to the Union commander. He told Bill to remain at headquarters for a few days. "I have something coming up very soon," he said, "and it is something I would not ask every man to do."

Within the week Bill learned what the "something" was. He was to be one of a handful of special scouts detailed to get into enemy territory. They were to discover Confederate strength in the region and, if possible, Confederate plans.

This looked to be more like spying than scouting. Being a spy-scout was possibly the most dangerous job in the army. If Hickok hadn't guessed as much already, he soon found out.

On the same day he received his assignment,

Bill rode toward Confederate Arkansas. He was dressed in clothes such as a farmer might wear. A week later he was on the Arkansas River where, as if by mere chance, he fell in with a camp of Rebel soldiers. He pretended to be a dull-witted farm hand who was trying to enlist on the Southern side.

The Rebel soldiers had a good time with Hickok. They jollied him along, and he took everything in good nature. He helped chop wood for their camp fires, lugged water for their cooks, and continued to ask for a chance to enlist.

This went on for two weeks, during which time Hickok learned a good deal about the number of Confederate troops along the Arkansas. As soon as he could learn something more about supplies, Bill figured he would disappear and make his way back to the Union lines. General Samuel Curtis, he was sure, would be glad of the information he was accumulating.

It didn't work out that way. On the day before he planned to take off, an officer and four

soldiers walked into the tent where Bill was
playing cards with comrades. The officer came to
the point.

"Are you Bill Hickok?" he asked.

Bill was almost but not quite stricken speech-
less. "No, my name is Jed Harris," he replied.

"That's strange. A corporal in my company
knew you at Fort Leavenworth as Bill Hickok."

"But . . ."

"And Bill Hickok is known to be with General
Curtis' headquarters."

"There must be some mistake," was all Hickok
could think of.

"The only mistake is yours—in being here,"
said the officer. "You are under arrest as a spy.
Take him, men. Tie his wrists, too."

Within an hour Hickok had been court-mar-
tialed and found guilty. Then Bill heard the
classic and fatal words—words he had read in
history books. "Bill Hickok," said the court officer, "I sentence you to be shot at sunrise."

And they led Union spy Hickok away to a

stout log cabin where he was to be held overnight—until sunrise.

Here, thought Bill, was the tightest fix he had
ever been in. Well, perhaps it wasn't any worse
than that time on the Santa Fe trail with the
she-grizzly. But it *was* worse, he came to think.
With the bear, he still had a chance. Here in
the guard-house, with soldiers walking post outside, he could see no chance at all.

There was no light in the cabin. The night
was dark enough. The best Bill could do was
to feel his way around the room. There was
one window, well barred, and the door. Nothing
else. The door felt as though it were fastened
with some sort of homemade lock. It might be
tampered with, if he had something to do the
tampering. But there wasn't anything.

During the night a thundering great storm
came up. Rain beat upon the cabin. Lightning
flashed again and again. With every flash Bill's
eyes were inspecting some part of his cell. At last
he saw something.

Protruding from a deep augur-hole in one of the logs was the handle of a common case-knife, such as was used at table. It was no bowie, no weapon. It had obviously been used for opening the cabin door from the inside, when the cabin was a home and not a guard-house; and it had been overlooked.

Moving carefully, Bill managed to pull the knife from its place. He took it to a corner of the cabin. Ramming the handle into a crevice between two logs to hold it, he started sawing the rope that bound his wrists by rubbing it to and fro across the blade.

It was a woefully dull blade, yet in half an hour Bill's hands were free. He lost no time, but started whetting the blade on the leather of his boots. This was to be desperate business. The blade must be keen. He stroked on and on, feeling the blade now and then with a thumb. Then he whetted it some more.

At last the blade felt keen enough. Wild Bill went to the door. He called to the guard. "I'm

powerful sick," he said. The guard opened
the door and stepped in. Bill grabbed him by
the hair with his left hand, and with the other
cut the man's throat.

The poor guard had started to cry out,
but the rolling thunder drowned the noise. The
other guards, in a shed some forty feet from the
cabin, heard nothing but the storm.

Working fast, Bill stripped the dead man and
put on his clothes. Then, picking up the rifle
which had fallen to the floor, Bill stepped out-

side. He closed the door, and began walking the post. He could hear the other guards talking and laughing in the shed.

For another ten minutes Wild Bill walked his post around the cabin. Then, just after a bright flash and while the thunder still boomed, he struck out into the brush a hundred yards off. The guards were still talking as he gained the woods and disappeared.

7: Hickok, the Union Spy

WILD BILL TRAVELED THE REST OF THE
night, then hid in the woods throughout the daylight hours. When night came, he was on
the move again. By morning he had found the
troops of General Curtis, and was soon in that
officer's tent, giving him information as to the

strength of the Confederate forces in the neighborhood.

Some of Bill's information concerned a large powder works which the Confederates had established at Yellville, Arkansas. More than a thousand men were engaged there in making explosives. General Curtis immediatedly ordered a detachment to raid Yellville. Wild Bill led the raid, which was successful. After a short battle, the Confederates were driven from the town, and the Union troops proceeded to burn the powder works and storehouses. They also captured some five hundred rifles, and more than a hundred horses.

General Curtis cited Wild Bill again for his great work.

During the next two years, Bill had several pretty tough assignments, sometimes as scout, again as a spy. Only once was he hit by a bullet, and from this he recovered quickly.

Late in 1863 he was in good shape again, and reported for duty. The duty turned out to be his enlisting as a soldier in the Confederate forces under General Steele. Bill asked to take one companion with him, an old friend named John W. Allen. The two men had served together on many expeditions. Bill knew Allen as a wonderful scout, good in a pinch.

The first thing Hickok and Allen did was to buy two sets of ragged old clothes from a farmer. Then they rode to Camden, Arkansas, where Confederate General Steele had his headquarters. They asked the way to the recruiting station, and soon the sergeant in charge looked up to see two hillbillies shuffle awkwardly into his office. They stood there staring, saying not a word.

"What do you want?" asked the sergeant.

"Want to git into the army," said Hickok.

"Want to be a sojer," said Allen.

The sergeant was amused. These two lads had evidently heard about the war between the states, and at last had come down from the hills to enlist. The Confederate fired questions at them so fast that they became rattled. Their funny answers threw the sergeant and some soldiers standing about into an uproar.

But the two hillbillies took everything in good spirit, and were soon given regular uniforms and sworn in. They were assigned to the Rebel cavalry. Had the sergeant been told that one of these rustics was the feared spy, Wild Bill Hickok, he doubtless would not have believed it.

Hickok and Allen were now members of the force under Confederate General Steele. This army was preparing to invade the region held by Union troops around Prairie d'Ane. For three months, the army moved slowly this way, then that, without any major engagement. But at last, one April day in 1864, General Steele put his entire force into battle formation. His artillery was unlimbered and went into action, hurling shells at the Union entrenchments.

For a week past Hickok had been looking for a chance by which he and Allen might leave the Rebels and get back to the Union Army. He had

gained much information as to the Rebel
strength, the number of troops, and even the
number of cannon available. Now he should
take this information to the Union commander.
But no opportunity had come.

When at last General Steele formed his battal-
ions for what seemed sure to be a real engagement, Bill decided the time had come for the
getaway. He sought out Allen.

"John, I've been thinking that this is it," said
Bill. "What do you think?"

"Maybe it's a chance," Allen replied. "We sure
ain't had any chances before."

"Are you willing to try it?"

"Yes, ready. What do we do?"

"All I can think of is to get on our horses,"
Hickok suggested. "Watch for a chance. Then
ride through this Rebel army as fast as we can."

"It's taking a big chance."

"I know it, John. But I can't see any
other way."

"I'm game," Allen agreed. "Any old time."

Suddenly, the Confederate troops were astonished to see two of their number ride out from their lines. Two officers, suspecting what was afoot, leaped to their saddles and started to give chase, followed by other horsemen.

It was going to be a hot ride. Allen and Hickok were away to a good start, however, and gaining. Then, when it appeared they were almost in the clear, both their horses stopped dead short of a deep and wide ditch.

Wild Bill wheeled his animal expertly. So did Allen. The two horses pounded forward again, and sailed into the air in superb leaps. Just then a shot from a pursuer struck Allen in mid-flight, and he fell from his horse like a stone.

While still in the air, Wild Bill turned in his saddle, revolver in hand, and fired twice. Two Rebel officers fell from their horses. It was unbelievable shooting, and a cheer went up from the Union soldiers who saw it happen.

On went Bill's horse straight for the Union lines. He was in the clear.

Blue-coated soldiers surrounded Hickok as he dismounted from his animal. The lads wanted to escort him to the tent of their commander. Bill wouldn't let them. "I'd rather you found a way to get poor Johnny Allen's body back to our lines," he told them. "I played in luck. Brave Johnny didn't."

The escape of two Union spies apparently had an effect on the Confederates. General Steele almost immediately gave the order for his troops to withdraw. The projected battle never began.

By now the great struggle between the North and South was all but ended. A few weeks later General Lee surrendered to General Grant, and the troops went home.

War's end found Bill Hickok in Springfield, Missouri, and it was here, on a hot day in July of 1865, that he took part in an affair that added to his growing reputation.

In Springfield was a man named Dave Tutt who had deserted the Confederate Army to serve as a spy for the Union. He and Wild Bill had been on several expeditions together. They had been good friends. Bill always spoke of Tutt as a brave man and a truly wonderful marksman.

What started the rift between these two friends appears to have been a woman, Susanna Moore. Both men had been courting her, and Wild Bill seems to have made more of an impression on the young lady than Tutt. Bad blood arose. It was soon to be spilled.

Dave Tutt had been sounding off to the effect that the next time he laid eyes on Hickok he was going to shoot him. Hickok had been warned of this by friends. He remarked that he did not want any trouble with Tutt. "This town ought to be big enough for both of us," he said. He sent word to Tutt that if he would keep to the west side of the public square, he, Hickok, would stay on the east side.

Possibly this message encouraged Tutt to think that Hickok was afraid of him. If so, it was a most fatal error.

The battle took place on the public square. Hickok was standing talking with a couple of friends on the street east of the common. He saw Tutt come out of the livery stable on the west side. Bill watched, casually, never thinking that Tutt would cross the square.

But Tutt now turned and struck out briskly across the center of the square. Bill called to him.

"Dave," said Bill, "you better not come across there."

By then Tutt was halfway across. He did not reply to Bill's warning, other than to draw and shoot.

Tutt's bullet whistled past Hickok's head. Wild Bill drew his gun, rested it across his left arm, and shot Dave Tutt through the heart. The man reeled, and fell where he stood. He had been killed at seventy-five yards.

Hickok walked directly across the square and into the courthouse. There he turned his gun over to the sheriff. "I just had to kill Dave Tutt," he said. "It was either him or me."

The sheriff placed Bill under arrest. The trial was brief. The jury, when shown the empty shell in Tutt's gun and having heard witnesses swear that Tutt had fired first, promptly freed Hickok.

The shooting of Dave Tutt was a sensation in Springfield. No few blamed Hickok for it, no matter what the jury said or did. Thanks to the late William E. Connelley, however, the record is quite clear. Mr. Connelley, Wild Bill Hickok's most careful biographer, went to great pains to learn the truth about the Hickok-Tutt affair. He wrote that all evidence pointed to Tutt as the aggressor; he had been purposely picking quarrels with Hickok for many weeks previous to the shooting.

Wild Bill remained in Springfield for several months more; but, like almost all other young men of the day, he seemed to be taken with a great restlessness. Over on the other side of the hill, beyond the mountain, across the river, somewhere surely the grass was greener, taller, thicker, sweeter, than it was where he stood. Mostly, during the period right after the big war, the new land of promise was believed to be in the American West.

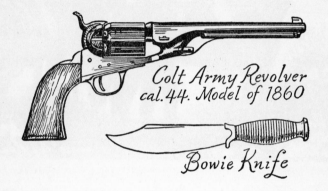

Colt Army Revolver
cal. 44. Model of 1860

Bowie Knife

8: Scouting for Custer

THE END OF THE CIVIL WAR BROUGHT ON A
new and great surge westward. The Homestead
Act had become law. A western farm or ranch
appealed to thousands of young men in the East
who had been cut loose from home ties by the
war.

One hundred and sixty acres of land could be

had free, if you would settle on it and make certain improvements. A man could also buy land cheap enough from the railroads which were threading the West in every direction.

This was all new country, a place where a young man could have his own home on his own land. It sounded like heaven to many thousands of ex-soldiers, and on they came to stake their claims.

As in every great migration, most of the emigrants were honest and hard-working people. Yet there were many others who came West with the single thought of preying upon the industrious. The ending of the war set these evil characters in motion, and they, too, found something of a heaven in the new West.

Of law there was little or none; that would have to wait until states and counties and towns were organized, taxes collected, and officials elected. Often, too, there was little law even then. Free and easy, every man for himself—that was the style of the time and place.

There still remained another danger added to that of the lawless emigrants to the West; the Indians had become desperate, and with good reason. Time after time a tribe was herded onto a reservation and ordered to remain there. Then, a year or two later, they were removed from the reservation and herded elsewhere, usually on much poorer land.

During the Civil War, when the country was wholly armed, Union troops had held the Indians in check. Now, in the late 1860s, there were few troops but just as many Indians as ever. Many chieftains thought the time had come for the tribes to strike.

So, they struck. There was no general uprising yet, though that would come; but a raid here, another raid there. Horses belonging to the white newcomers were run off. Barns were burned. The few troops now on the plains were constantly harassed.

It was probably inevitable that Wild Bill Hickok should take part in these minor if bloody wars. In any case, Bill's first job after the Civil War was that of a United States deputy marshal. After receiving this commission, he was assigned to the Army post of Fort Riley, Kansas.

Fort Riley was in bad shape. Discipline of the troops had broken down completely. Desertions were rife. The soldiers were thought to be working with horse thieves, both red and white, and with other crooks. In one month no less than eighty-four Army horses had "disappeared" from the Fort. Nobody seemed to have any idea where they had gone.

Hickok's wide acquaintance in Kansas and with old friends almost everywhere in the state gave him a big advantage. He could learn things no regular Army man could possibly learn. After only two days at Fort Riley, most of which he spent talking with Indians in and out of the post, Hickok rode away alone. Six days later he returned to the Fort, bringing nine Army mules and two deserters.

Taking his ease for a day, Bill asked for

a party of four men, got them, and struck out up the Solomon Valley. He and his four troopers soon returned. This time they were driving more than two hundred Army horses and mules. *But they brought back no prisoners.*

This oddity took the interest of General Winfield Scott Hancock, who asked Wild Bill to report to him.

"Marshal Hickok," said the general, "did you find these Army animals loose on the prairie, or were they in somebody's possession?"

"Oh," said Bill, "I'm not sure about that, but we did find some bad-looking characters around there."

"Around where?"

"Up the valley a piece."

"Didn't they object to your recovering the horses?" the general asked.

"They didn't seem too pleased."

The general laughed. "They were not pleased, you say?"

"No, not exactly."

General Hancock tried to pin Bill down: what had happened? How had Bill and four men retrieved all these animals from horse thieves so quickly? Had there been no shooting? Wild Bill clammed up tighter than ever.

"They sort of tried to stop us," was all he would say, "but they didn't. And they're not likely to trouble you any more."

Not a word more would Hickok say. The four troopers, too, were oddly uncommunicative. The incident remains one of many in Hickok's life about which little or nothing is known. He was one of the shyest men in the West. When plagued about it he always replied: "There's plenty of good talkers without me, and a whole lot too many windjammers."

However he accomplished it, Bill Hickok had cleaned out a crew of notable horse thieves, and had also cured a number of soldiers of the same stripe. Discipline at Fort Riley showed a vast improvement.

Just in time. The plains suddenly erupted in a

genuine war with the Indians. Sioux and Coman-
ches were on the prowl. Warriors of the Cheyenne, Kiowa, and other warlike tribes who had
made peace with the whites joined the excitement. Settlements and isolated ranches were attacked. Butchery followed.

General Hancock knew who was needed.
He asked that General George Armstrong Custer
be assigned to his command. This dashing young
officer had made a brilliant record in the Civil
war; and now he came to the plains to be in
command of all cavalry in the campaign. The
army posts used included Forts Riley, Hays,
McPherson, Larned, and two or three more.

The first thing Custer did on his arrival at
Fort Hays was to ask for a famous scout named
Wild Bill Hickok.

Hickok was happy with the assignment. It
would mean action. That was the kind of officer
Custer was.

Hickok's first duties seemed easy and simple
enough—to him. He carried dispatches from Cus-

ter to his troops scattered all over the plains. The country was seething with Indians. But Hickok knew Indians as well as he knew the country. He seemed to have little difficulty getting dispatches to and from Custer.

But then came that experience not far from Fort Sedgwick. One can doubt that Wild Bill, casual as he was about such things, ever forgot it.

Hickok had come across the trail of a large band of Indians, much larger than he or anyone else had thought were operating in the Fort Sedgwick neighborhood. Bill thought he should try to find where they had made camp and, if possible, their approximate strength.

The ground was hard, the trailing poor. When the sun faded that day, the trail faded, too. Night had come. Bill had to guess: "Which way from here, if I were a chief, would I take my band of warriors?" Bill chose the direction which he knew would lead him to a spot on a creek that was well hidden by low hills.

It was a little past midnight when the scout found that his guess had been correct. Through the dark he could see faintly the forms of many lodges, or tepees. There was only one small patch of light showing. Bill figured this came from the door-flap of the chief's lodge.

The chief, so Bill calculated, would be holding council with his leading warriors. It would be mighty nice to listen in. Bill spoke or understood most if not all of the jargons of the plains tribes. But could he somehow work his way undiscovered among the many lodges that surrounded the tepee whence came the light?

Wild Bill dismounted. He tethered his horse. He moved forward in the dark slowly, a step at a time. stopping to listen. He could hear the occasional stamping of a pony. He knew that a pony was tied at the door of every lodge. He knew, too, that there were no doubt a hundred dogs in camp, sleeping here and there in the grass. The snort of one or the bark of the other could rouse the whole camp.

Bill got down on his hands and knees, still moving forward, making his way gingerly between the many lodges. Now and again he could hear some brave snoring within a lodge. Once, a pony gave a start as Bill approached, but it did not snort or whinny.

At last Wild Bill arrived in the tall grass around the lodge of the chief. He crawled close and listened.

At first all he could make out was a word or a disconnected phrase that meant nothing to him. Then the council began to warm up. The voices grew louder.

For perhaps half an hour Bill listened while the warriors discussed their next move. He learned that these Indians were well acquainted with the strength of the Army troops at Fort Sedgwick. He discovered that they were in close communication with other tribes on the Upper Arkansas river.

On they talked, while Bill listened in amazement. These redskins must have some source of information within Fort Sedgwick itself! Who? It must be some Indian working in the Fort and fully trusted by the troops.

Hickok had learned all he needed to know. He began to work his way, most slowly, back toward the outskirts of the camp where his horse was waiting.

All went well until Bill had got to the very last lodge along his way. Here he stood up and stretched. Just then a tall warrior emerged from the door of a lodge. He stopped. He saw that this stranger was an intruder, a white man. He acted quickly. Without word or grunt he drew a knife and lunged at Bill. The scout drew back, pulled his own knife and attacked, driving the long blade deep into the brave's chest.

Although not a word had been spoken, the silent battle had aroused the sleeping dogs. They came running and barking, making a din that woke the whole village.

Out of the surrounding lodges poured Indians; braves and squaws. They were shouting, "Pawnee! Pawnee! Watch horses!"

None of the braves attacked Hickok. They did not see him. They believed Pawnees were on a raid to steal horses, and they mounted their own ponies and dashed wildly around the village, looking for the attackers.

Well, there was Wild Bill enclosed by two hundred or more Indian braves seeking the source of danger. He had no chance to reach his own horse.

Just then one of the braves came up on his pony, and as he passed, Bill took an enormous chance, a last chance. With an agile leap, the scout landed square on the pony's back close behind the warrior.

The astounded Indian started to turn. Wild Bill's knife was out. He plunged it into the brave's heart and pushed him off the running horse. Then he joined in the circle dashing around and around the village.

The Indians still knew nothing of Wild Bill's presence. On they went, pounding in a circle around the lodges. On the next trip around, Bill urged his horse out of the parade and toward the open country. He had disappeared before the Indians discovered one of their comrades dead on the grass, another dead close beside his own tepee.

Wild Bill rode his saddleless pony throughout the night. At daybreak he was at the Fort, where he reported to Colonel Lindsay. It had been as narrow an escape as Wild Bill was used to.

Scout Hickok continued to serve throughout the Indian War of the latter 1860s, performing feats of daring and endurance that General Custer hailed as almost without comparison. Custer also had something to say of Hickok's appearance.

"The most prominent of my scouts," wrote the famous Indian fighter, "was Wild Bill

Wild Bill's knife was out.

Hickok. He was a Plainsman in every sense of the word. He was six feet one inch, with broad shoulders, a face strikingly handsome, and a sharp, clear blue eye which stared you straight in the face. His hair and complexion were those of a perfect blond. In his dress, he blended the neatness of the dandy with the extravagant taste and style of the frontiersman."

In 1869 General Custer and his brave troops, including Scout Hickok, subdued the no-less-brave Indians; and a temporary peace followed. The tribes were to rise again. Indeed, the tribes were finally to kill Custer. But Wild Bill's Indian-fighting days ceased with the end of the 1860s.

One more incident, however, belongs to this period in Hickok's life. At the request of United States Senator Henry Wilson, Wild Bill guided a senatorial party on an expedition that opened the eyes of the Easterners to the new empire of the West. On their return to Fort Hays, a banquet was given in Hickok's honor, and he was presented with a pair of ivory-handled revolvers. These he was to carry the rest of his life.

With the Indians under control, at least for a time, the greatest danger to human life and property in the West was to come from dishonest and criminal white adventurers. These people were flocking to the new towns and giving the region its deserved name of the "wild and woolly" West. Wild Bill was ready to change his career to meet the new conditions.

9: Taming a Wild Town

NEAR FORT HAYS IN KANSAS WAS THE SETTLE-
ment called Hays City, a depot for the trade
with Santa Fe, and a center to which thousands
of men came to blow off steam and have what
they thought of as a good time. The streets were
lighted at night by the blazing lights of saloons
and dance halls.

95

In 1869, Hays City also contained many decent, hard-working people, but they had completely lost control. What today we call gangsters had taken over. They were running Hays City for the benefit of themselves and the members of their gangs.

We must remember that settlement of the West was going forward so rapidly that laws and courts could not begin to keep up. They would come in time, of course, but meanwhile this fringe of the farthest frontier was open range for criminals. Meanwhile, too, honest settlers defended themselves and their property as best they could.

The honest citizens of Hays City seemed to be fighting a losing battle. Murders were so frequent, and violence so common, that a citizens' committee had been unable to find a man who cared to risk his life as city marshal. Then it occurred to one of the people that here, at the nearby Fort, was one of the best-known scouts and fighters of the plains; namely, Wild Bill

Hickok. Possibly he would make a first-class peace officer. A delegation of citizens called on Bill at the Fort and invited him to take the office. Wild Bill had no other plans. He accepted.

As marshal of Hays City, Wild Bill added one item to his usual arsenal of two revolvers and bowie-knife. He bought a shotgun, sawed off much of the barrel, and patrolled the streets with the weapon slung over one arm.

It was Bill's custom to drop into one saloon after another, and to talk with the proprietors and customers. He seldom accepted a drink. Now and again he would join in a game of poker. He always sat with his back to the wall, facing the main entrance.

His first month on the job passed quietly, for just the announcement of his arrival as peace officer seemed to have a sobering effect on Hays City. His reputation was such that a soft word from him served to calm drunks who had turned dangerous. He stopped many saloon fights merely by stepping between the opponents before either could draw gun. This was dangerous work. But week followed week and still Wild Bill had not drawn a revolver, or even used his shotgun.

One of the worst characters in town was a desperado called Jack Strawhan. He was also a bully who wanted to have the reputation of being a bad man with a gun, a real killer, a man to leave strictly alone. He was heard to remark that "this Hickok" was pretty much of a bluff. One day in Chris Riley's saloon Strawhan felt the urge to talk some more.

"One of these days," announced Bad-man Strawhan, "I am going to call Hickok's bluff."

"Mister," said Riley, "you better think twice before you take on Marshal Hickok."

"Yeah—think three or mebbe four times," added a bystander.

"That so?" Bad-man Strawhan drew his big knife and casually picked his teeth. "All I got to say is that you keep your eyes open and you'll see. I aim to run him out of town."

A few days later the encounter took place. Wild Bill was standing in Drum's saloon, his back partly toward the door. He saw Strawhan come in. Bill never turned. The desperado thought he was unnoticed. A good chance. He could shoot Hickok from behind.

Strawhan drew his gun and raised it to aim— and probably never knew what hit him. Without turning his head, but looking into the big mirror behind the bar, Wild Bill drew and fired in a split second, aiming over his shoulder. The bullet caught Strawhan in the middle of the forehead. He was dead when he struck the floor.

Wild Bill's backward shot created a sensation. News of it spread up and down Hays City's main street. Men came running to Drum's saloon until it was packed to the doors.

That evening, while friends kept Bill's attention with conversation, the town band formed and at the head of a procession of hundreds of cheering citizens, paraded up the street. Outside the marshal's office, it stopped to serenade Wild

Bill Hickok, the officer who had tamed one of the wildest towns in the West.

But Hays City, though much better than it had been, was not quite cleaned up. In the thousands of characters who flowed into and out of town every few days, there were many who resented any sort of order.

One night, as Marshal Hickok was making his rounds, a man stepped suddenly from a dark doorway, cocked gun in hand, and covered him.

"Hickok, I got you now," said the stranger. "I'll give you one minute to say your prayers."

"Well, well," Bill remarked in mild surprise. "It sure looks as though you had me this time." Then, looking over the thug's shoulder, he cried: "Don't hit him, Andy!" The man instantly turned to see who was behind him. Wild Bill shot him dead.

The whole affair from start to finish did not occupy more than thirty seconds. When news of it got around, most of the local crooks made up their minds: they must either reform their ways or leave Hays City.

One disturbing element remained, however. This was a group of rowdy soldiers from nearby Fort Hays. Their leader was Lieutenant Tom Custer, the brother of General Custer, and he and his gang did not believe they could be arrested by civilian officers such as Marshal Hickok.

A favorite pastime of these soldier rowdies was to ride through the town at great speed while shooting with both hands. Hickok sent word to Lieutenant Custer, politely advising him to stop the practice.

On the very next night, Custer returned with his crew. This time, just to show what they thought of Marshal Hickok, they shot up a saloon—every window in it, as well as the bar mirror.

Wild Bill talked the matter over with city officials. "I hate to arrest a brother of General

Custer's," he said. "But this young squirt is going
too far."

"Arrest him, then," said the mayor.

"I will, but I want to be certain first that he
will get a stiff fine for disorderly conduct."

"You bring him in and I'll see to that," said
the police court judge.

"It's a deal," Wild Bill said.

He didn't have to wait long. That night Custer
and a dozen soldiers rode into town. First they
got drunk. They shot out a window or two. Then
Custer rode his horse into a billiard hall.
The proprietor ran to get Hickok. The marshal
hurried to the hall to find it surrounded by a
big crowd. Bill pushed his way forward and
stepped inside. Just then Custer was trying
to make his horse leap onto a billiard table. The
animal refused.

"Custer, that horse knows more than you do,"
Wild Bill cried above the hubbub. "Get down!
Then get out of here."

Custer made another attempt. Without a word

Wild Bill grabbed the horse's bridle. The animal reared and pulled away, kicking and thrashing, trampling down two men. Bill drew a gun and shot the poor beast through the head.

Custer fell to the floor. Bill took him by the collar. He jerked him to his feet. He slapped handcuffs on the soldier's wrists. "Now," said he quietly, "you are under arrest. Come with me."

Custer was meek enough now. And the police judge was as good as his word. He found Custer guilty and fined him a hundred dollars. Custer and his sobered crew returned to the Fort.

But Hickok wasn't through yet with the rowdy soldiers. Two nights later Custer and three extra-bad men who had spent most of their Army lives in guardhouses, came quietly into Hays City. They made enquiries, and learned that Wild Bill was then in the Mint saloon. They tied their horses outside and went in.

The Mint was so poorly lighted that it was almost impossible to tell one person from another. Dense smoke added to the gloom. Before

Wild Bill knew what was afoot, one of Custer's thugs leaped on Bill's shoulders. Another pinioned Bill's arms. But Bill got one arm free.

One arm was enough. With it Bill drew gun and fired backward over his shoulder. The soldier fell from Bill's back. He was dead.

Bill now shot the third soldier, who stood in front of him, gun in hand.

Next, Bill turned his revolver on the man who still clung to his other arm from behind. That fellow too went down.

Tom Custer had kept out of the affray. He dodged out of the saloon as the last of his bullies went down to stay.

Wild Bill stood there, cool as ice, smoking gun in hand, curls of powder smoke wafting around him, waiting to see if there were any others present who wanted action. There were none. Bill put away his revolver.

The sensational killing of three toughs in less than three minutes was like nothing else anyone in Hays City had ever seen. Wild Bill himself said he greatly regretted the incident. "But it was either me," said he, "or them."

Men who witnessed Wild Bill's all but incredible performance with the soldiers never forgot it to their last day. They told the story over and over again, in saloons all over the West, in corrals, in ranch houses, around camp fires, and in jolting stage coaches. Wild Bill had been well-known before the affair. Now he was famous.

The quick removal of three undesirable characters seemed to sober the soldiers at Fort Hays. It had a like effect on Hays City. Something like order, if not formal law, had come to this frontier settlement.

Where all had been chaos before, life and property were now respected. A newspaperman who visited Hays City at this period wrote that violence was a thing of the past. He credited Marshal Hickok for this condition. Even in New York and Boston, people were reading about the fearless peace officer of Hays City, Kansas.

Late in 1869, Hickok asked to resign as

marshal. He said that he needed some rest for his job had kept him constantly on the alert. He was beginning to feel the strain. It had been in his mind, he said, to spend the winter quietly in Topeka, the state capital.

Although citizens did not like to lose this man who had done so much in so short a time for their town, they appreciated his desire, and they rallied to give him a big send-off. Bill arrived at Topeka on New Year's Day of 1870.

It was to be a pleasant interlude. Many old friends were in the town, including Buffalo Bill Cody. The two Bills spent much time together, standing around the local corrals, discussing horses; and like all old soldiers, they fought over again the Indian campaigns in which both men had taken part.

They played some poker and faro. At least once Wild Bill gave an exhibition of his marksmanship. Buffalo Bill took his hat from his head and sailed it high into the air. As the headpiece curved in an erratic arc, Wild Bill, a gun in each hand, shot a row of holes along the out-side of the rim. When the hat fell to the ground, the holes were found to be as evenly spaced as if they had been punched by hand.

Shooting such as this was one of several reasons why Wild Bill Hickok had survived ten years of as dangerous a life as any man is likely to know. He was going to need his uncanny skill with firearms in his next job, which was soon to appear.

10: Abilene Was Tough

A MAN OF OUTSTANDING COURAGE AND ABIL-
ity like Wild Bill Hickok was sure to be in
demand in the West until the last desperate character had been removed from the scene.

Bill's taming of lawless Hays City seemed little
short of a miracle. His iron will had held at
bay all the vicious and unbridled characters who

sought to live by violence. Why, it was marvel-
lous. And it had happened, while men watched,
in Hays City, Kansas. The very thought of it
gave hope to the decent men and women who
were settling the American frontier.

Meanwhile, in other parts of the West, honest
people still lived in fear, just as had been the
case in Hays City before Marshal Hickok took
charge. Now that Hays City had become an or-
derly place to which outlaws and criminals gave
wide berth, perhaps the worst settlement on the
plains was Abilene, also in Kansas.

Abilene was at the northern end of the Chis-
holm Trail. It was the southern terminus of the
Kansas Pacific Railroad.

To Abilene from Texas each year came
immense droves of cattle. These were sorted at
Abilene and then put aboard cars for shipment
to the great meat-packing centers of Chicago and
Cincinnati.

Five thousand cow hands often gathered in Abilene to celebrate completion of the roundup.

Another five thousand people made up the city's more or less permanent population.

One hundred and ten saloons, hotels, dance halls and gambling places stood side by side on Abilene's streets. The whole town was baited with card games and other forms of gambling and trickery to catch the simple cow hand and remove his cash.

There were also crooks who preferred the quicker methods of murder and robbery.

Abilene had grown up riotously around the end of the railroad. Stockyards ran for miles. So did the sidetracks. Three brass bands had been organized. So had a fire department. There was a lively newspaper. The roaring town had thought of almost everything except a police department.

During the summer and fall of 1870, more than thirty men were murdered in Abilene, six of them during five minutes of gunplay in the Bull's Head Saloon.

Others had been shot in saloons named the

Alamo, the Sidetrack, the Lone Jag, and the Gold Room.

When the better citizens at last began to realize their town had been taken over and was being ruled by gangsters, they hurriedly appointed a city marshal. This was Tom Smith, a very brave man, who set out to do for Abilene what Hickok had done for Hays City. But bravery alone wasn't enough. Within a short time of his appointment, Marshal Smith was waylaid one night and shot to death.

Abilene's underworld let it be known that Abilene would not tolerate an officer.

In another effort to bring some sort of order to the place, the citizens elected Joseph McCoy mayor. Mayor McCoy was an honest and energetic man. On the day he took office he called the city council together. "Gentlemen," said he, "it is obvious we must get an officer who not only is fearless, but who is quicker on the draw than any of these professional badmen who have flocked to our city."

"There's only one man who fills that bill," said a member of the council. "And that's Hickok."

"Hickok?" said the Mayor. "I read in the paper that he's in Kansas City this week, visiting friends."

"Reckon we could get him to come to Abilene?" another council member asked.

"I propose," said Mayor McCoy, "to take the train to Kansas City tonight. I'll see Wild Bill tomorrow and offer him the job of city marshal of Abilene at a hundred and fifty dollars a month."

"You can't get him for that money."

"Just a moment," put in McCoy. "I hadn't quite finished. I'll offer him a hundred and fifty dollars a month—plus half the fines collected in our police court."

The city council agreed.

Four days later Wild Bill was saying good-bye to Kansas City friends. He had bought a new suit and several white shirts with pleated fronts. These were to become his trademark. He wore this type of shirt ever after.

On the next night, as the Kansas Pacific's train pulled into Abilene, a tall erect man who wore his yellow hair tumbling down over his shoulders, and carried a large valise, got off the cars. From there he walked to the shack called City Hall. On his way uptown Wild Bill also got a look at the town he had been hired to tame and civilize.

Lights blazed for blocks. Cow hands were riding up and down the wide streets, sending up dust in clouds. Every now and then one of them shot wildly into the air. Dogs ran through the streets, barking. Men and women stumbled drunkenly out of lighted doorways, some of them falling on the plank walks. Passersby paid them no attention, merely walking around them.

The night was raucous from the pounding of

a score of pianos. From the many dance halls came the tooting of bands and the stomping of feet.

As Bill was walking past one of the larger and noisier of these places, a window suddenly crashed and through it tumbled a man who was waving a revolver. He leaped to his feet and emptied his gun through the broken window, then ran down a nearby alley.

Wild Bill went on to the City Hall. The mayor and councilmen gave him a hearty welcome. "There is plenty of work for you to do here," said Mayor McCoy.

"So I judged on the way from the depot," Bill said humorously. "Is this about an average evening?"

"No," replied the mayor, "it's really somewhat quiet for us. Only a few cow hands in town."

"Perhaps I'd better get me a room and some rest," Bill remarked. "I aim to take over tomorrow and I want to feel fit and proper."

The new marshal of Abilene went to sleep

that night to the music of many pianos and bands and the occasional sound of gunfire and yelling.

During the daylight hours of his first day in Abilene Marshal Hickok sat quietly in several saloons, playing cards, talking with the proprietors and customers. He was planning to make his official appearance after supper, when the town began to wind up and get going.

So, that evening, as Abilene started filling with cow hands and assorted characters typical of the West, the new marshal walked out of his office and into the very center of the main street. He carried his usual side-arms, and a bowie knife. Over one arm was the sawed-off shotgun he always carried but seldom seemed to find use for.

Wild Bill knew very well the whole town was agog that he had come there to tame the place. There had been talk of little else all day.

Bill thought that the trouble-makers should be shown right off that he feared no man. On his first night of duty, he proceeded to stroll casually down the middle of the main street to the railroad depot, then turned around and strolled from the depot to the Last Chance saloon on the city's outskirts. Then he went back to City Hall.

It was probably a reckless thing to do, but Bill defended his action by saying it was the best and quickest way to tell the crooks he meant business.

His only effort on the first night was to stop some mounted cow hands who were shooting into the air. "Boys," he said, "I wish you wouldn't do that. I hate the sound of gunfire."

The cow hands were so astounded that they put away their guns and went around telling everybody that the new city marshal did not like noise.

A few nights later, when Bill had asked a bunch of cow hands to put away their guns, two of them refused and called Hickok a bad name. Wild Bill simply took hold of the two roisterers and knocked their heads together. "Now go home," he told them.

Next morning these two men, who were still drunk, got a gallon of whiskey and started recruiting a gang to ride with them into town, take Wild Bill, and hang him. That, they said, would be notice that Abilene was a cow-hands' town where cow hands could do as they pleased.

The gang grew by the hour. By mid-afternoon, more than a hundred wild and half-drunk young men were getting up steam for the trip to town. But one of their number, who knew Wild Bill and had seen him in action at Hays City, quietly walked away from the growing gang, got onto his horse, and rode into Abilene. He looked up Hickok and warned him what was afoot.

"Thank you, son," said the marshal. "I'm glad you let me know. Say nothing to anybody. I'll be ready for the gang when they get here."

Late in the afternoon, Wild Bill strolled to the Last Chance saloon, on the edge of town. It stood by the trail over which the cow hands must come into Abilene. Bill said nothing to the Last Chance's proprietor about what was up. He merely passed the time of day and watched the play at a faro table for a few minutes, meanwhile keeping an ear cocked.

After a while Bill heard the pounding of horses' hoofs out on the prairie. Shotgun in hand, he stepped out of the saloon, and there in front of the building he stood, motionless, waiting for the bad boys of Abilene.

On came the troop of cow hands. Possibly they saw the lone man there in front of the saloon, and thought nothing of it. But as they came abreast of him, up went the shotgun to the ready.

"Clear out!" called the city marshal loud and clear.

The leading riders pulled their horses to a stop, while those in the rear piled headlong into the foremost.

"Clear out, I say!" Again the order rang out, and the sawed-off shotgun moved up and down.

"Clear out!" called the city marshal.

Confusion hit the mounted ranks. The leaders wheeled, and started back whence they had come, the others after them, all riding furiously to get away from the lone man poised with the shotgun. Wild Bill did not trouble to fire a shot after them.

By nightfall, the news of Bill's stopping one hundred horsemen and making them turn tail was all over town. It was reckoned a wonderful joke on the wild young cow hands.

The event seemed also to have had a quieting effect on Abilene. For better than a month, Marshal Hickok found little to do other than to remind cow hands and others that shooting firearms, even in sport, was forbidden by city ordinance.

Bill also asked the proprietors of the Bull's Head saloon to keep better order in their place. He suggested, too, that they remove a vulgar sign that hung over the bar.

11: A Roundup Tragedy

THE OPERATORS OF THE BULL'S HEAD WERE two of the toughest Texans who ever came into Kansas. Ben Thompson had a long list of murders against his name. He was a bad man to offend.

His partner, a huge gambler named Phil

Coe, was known to be plenty quick, both with his temper and his gun. Their saloon was the biggest and best-equipped place in Abilene.

On the day after Wild Bill had warned Coe and Thompson to remove the vulgar sign, Bill strolled into the Bull's Head. The sign was right where it had been.

Bill walked up to Coe, who was standing behind the bar. "Mister Coe," Bill said without raising his voice, "I'll give you a couple of minutes to take that thing down."

"What's the matter with that sign?" Coe asked.

"It's against decency," said Bill, "and I say it is also against the law. Take it down—now."

Coe looked at Bill. Bill looked at Coe. For a long moment the two big men stared at each other. Then Coe muttered something, went to the wall, and took down the sign.

"Give it to me," said Wild Bill. Without a word Coe passed it to the marshal. Wild Bill broke it over his knee and put the pieces into the big stove. Then he walked out.

Big Phil Coe and Ben Thompson did not like to take orders from anybody, least of all from a peace officer. From the first, they had been planning how best to get rid of Hickok.

They knew too well that you couldn't just walk up to Hickok and shoot him. Many men had tried that, and they had been buried. No, that wouldn't do. It would be better to gang up on Hickok; perhaps stir up a drunken mob. Safer and surer that way. Perhaps.

Coe and Thompson were aware that roundup time was nearing in Abilene. The town would fill up and run over with wild men. Liquor would flow by the barrel-full. The faro banks and roulette wheels would operate day and night. Riot—that was a proper name to apply to the roundup in Abilene.

In such a crowd, there was bound to be much shooting, all in play, of course. There would be a heap of noise and excitement. At such a time, many things could be done. It was an idea. . . .

On the first night of the roundup, Wild Bill was eating supper while five—or perhaps it was six—thousand cow hands were riding into town from the many camps on the nearby prairie.

The merry-making started promptly. Wild Bill had reminded all saloon keepers there was to be no gunplay in town. "Tell the boys that," he had said. "Anything within reason goes. But no shooting."

As the night wore on, citizens were amazed at the result of Wild Bill's order. There was a great deal of noise, but no shooting. That is, no shooting up to about ten o'clock.

It was almost unbelievable that the word of one man should hold in check thousands of men on their biggest spree of the year. Wild Bill Hickok—there he stood now, serene and laughing, bantering with drunken cow hands and passing the time of day with criminals.

There he stood in front of the Novelty Thea-

ter and Saloon, his one deputy, trusted Mike
Williams, by his side, watching the Wild West at
play.

But trouble was hatching. Big Phil Coe was
not in his own saloon, where ordinarily he
would have been if he didn't have something
on his mind.

Coe was out in the streets, talking with the
cow hands and the enemies of law and order.
He stood for a while in front of the Alamo Saloon where a big crowd had congregated. Coe
was joking with the crowd, and there was purpose in his joking.

"It ain't like it used to be when cow hands
were real men," he said. "In those days a man
could celebrate the way he wanted to—like
this." Coe drew his Colts and fired into the
air.

Across the street at the Novelty, Wild Bill
heard this, the first shot of the evening. He
turned to his deputy. "Mike," he said, "you stay
here. I'll go over to the Alamo and see who is

getting out of control." He started across the wide street.

Wild Bill had no desire to prevent men from having fun. He knew, too, that shooting guns was considered good fun by cow hands on a spree.

Bill's order banning such shooting was for the purpose of discipline. Some sort of discipline was the next best thing to formal law, of which there was little in Kansas and none at all in Abilene. That is, there was no law except for Wild Bill's stated regulations.

Wild Bill, a master of men, knew that his ban on firearms must be enforced, and quickly. Either that, or he would soon lose the iron-handed control he had held over Abilene since his first night as city marshal.

Hickok went directly to the Alamo Saloon. There was a lot of smoke inside, but it came from tobacco, not powder. He walked out into the street. "Who fired that shot?" he demanded of anybody who cared to listen.

There was a moment of silence and suspense, then a big voice boomed out of the night. "I fired that shot." It was Big Phil Coe.

Before Wild Bill could move, a blast came out of the dark where Coe was standing. The bullet grazed Hickok's leg.

Wild Bill drew a revolver and fired just as Coe shot again. The two shots were simultaneous. Bystanders heard but one report.

Coe fell to the ground. He quickly raised up on one elbow and shot again. He missed.

In the two-second silence Wild Bill could hear guns being cocked all around him in the dark. These men, he knew, were Coe's friends, his gang.

Suddenly Bill noticed a figure coming toward him on the run. Bill fired. The shadowy figure's arms went into the air. Hickok shot again. The man fell.

Bill went forward and bent over. Bystanders heard him give a low cry. "My God! It's Mike Williams."

Mike it was, Wild Bill's own deputy. He had been coming on the run to help his chief.

Hickok was wild with grief. He lifted Williams from the ground, calling for somebody to get a doctor. By the time Bill had laid his friend on a table in the Alamo, poor Mike was dead.

Wild Bill's grief quickly turned to anger—a wild, unreasoning fury at the mobs of drunken men who were whooping it up in Abilene. Had it not been for them, Mike Williams would not have been killed. That was the way it seemed to Wild Bill. When he had unwittingly shot the good friend who had come to help him, Hickok had been in the midst of real danger.

He had known there were a score of men in that mob who wanted to kill him, Hickok. When a figure had come running through the dark, Bill naturally believed it to be one of Phil Coe's friends, coming to revenge the big Texan. So, Hickok had shot and shot to kill. . . .

It was one time Wild Bill regretted his expert marksmanship.

Looking at poor Mike Williams there on the faro table, Wild Bill wept.

Out in the streets, drunks had begun shooting. Wild Bill reloaded and wheeled the cylinders to make certain they were turning free and fast. Then he went outside.

He plunged into the midst of the mob, pushing men right and left. "Get out of town," he roared again and again. "Get out of here, all of you!"

Up and down Main Street he plowed through the crowds, crying, "Off the streets! Off the streets!"

Now he strode into the Alamo. "Clear the place!" he ordered the bartenders. "Get every man out of here! Blow out your lights! Lock your doors."

Out of the Alamo he went, and into the next place, a dance hall. Women screamed as Wild Bill came through the door, his eyes blazing, a cry on his lips. "Shut the joint! Out of here— all of you! Douse those lamps!"

Down one side of the street and up the other stalked City Marshal Hickok, a man crazed with grief and anger. One by one the lights went out. Doors closed. Shutters went up. All over town suddenly-sobered men were mounting their horses, getting out of Abilene.

Colonel Edward C. Little saw Wild Bill on his rounds that night. He never forgot it. "That night," the colonel recalled in later years, "that night Bill Hickok walked the town like a madman, and the desperate bullies hid in cellars and in the sunflower patches. Either that, or they got aboard their ponies and made their way back to the cattle camps."

By one o'clock in the morning, Abilene was as quiet as a cemetery. One man had cleared thousands of assorted cow hands and others from the streets, had shut every saloon and dance hall in the city. Now he went to the hotel where a doctor was working over the wounded Phil Coe.

"My father received wounds like mine," Coe said, "but he lived. So will I." But he was obviously dying even as he spoke. Wild Bill set out to find a clergyman and then led him to the room where Coe was sinking steadily.

Phil Coe died before morning. When the news came to Wild Bill he heard it with regret. "Coe was a brave man," Bill said, "I had to shoot him. He tried to shoot me. I was lucky."

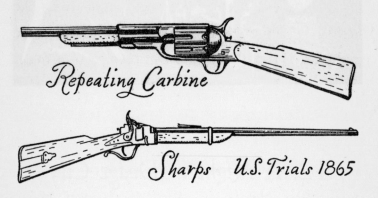

Repeating Carbine

Sharps U.S. Trials 1865

12: A Night in Dodge City

PERHAPS IT WAS THE TRAGEDY OF POOR MIKE
Williams that altered Wild Bill's thinking. It
may have been that and a combination of other
things. In any case, a change in Wild Bill's career was about to take place.

He asked to be relieved of his post as marshal
of Abilene. He was sick of the occupation. He

was tired of living always on the alert for trouble and danger. He wanted to get away from constant turmoil.

The good people of Abilene hated to see Bill leave. He had come to their town when it was probably the worst of all the border settlements. In a few months he had so tamed it that life and property were not only as safe there as in any other Western town, but much safer than in most.

As peace officer at Fort Riley and at Hays City he had done much the same for those once dangerous places.

Wild Bill Hickok had, in short, brought order to the most lawless region of North America. Now he would retire and find something less strenuous to do.

Or, that is the way Wild Bill planned it.

There are some people, however, who are seemingly marked for lives of action. Just before Bill took off from Abilene he received a letter from an old pal, Garibaldi Smith. After years of hard life on the plains, Smith had settled down in Dodge City, Kansas, to enjoy a quiet life.

But Dodge City, so Smith wrote Wild Bill, had developed certain characteristics of the older frontier towns. An underworld of crooked gamblers and robbers was beginning to feel strong enough to take over the place. The boss thug was known as Jake Jones.

In his letter to Hickok, Garibaldi Smith pleaded: "Can't you come here for a few days and put the fear of law and order into these cutthroats?"

Wild Bill had always liked Smith, who in the past had done him a number of favors. Little as he wanted to contend any more with the lawless elements, still, he would like to see Smith again; if, at the same time, he could be of any service to Dodge City, well . . .

Hickok arrived in Dodge City unannounced. Only Smith and the mayor knew he was coming. Smith related to Bill how the mayor had been trying to take action against the Jake Jones gang but had made little progress. The toughs were growing bolder.

Smith had just heard an ugly rumor, too. On that very night, he said, the gang leaders were planning to call in a body on the mayor, who ran a drug store. They would beat up the mayor, help themselves to his merchandise, and then wreck the store. This was to be a warning. If the mayor didn't heed the warning, the gang would return and hang him.

"Did you say a Jake Jones is the gang's leader?" asked Bill.

"Yep," Smith replied. "The same Jake we used to know around Hays City."

"I seem to recall that I ran him out of Hays City."

"You did," Smith assured his friend. "Don't you remember? He was running a crooked faro bank in the Birdcage saloon?"

"That's right," said Bill. "But when I told him to leave, he got out of Hays City like a good boy. No trouble."

"Maybe. But Jake is feeling his muscle here. He's killed two men in Dodge City. He's bad, I tell you."

"All right, then, let's see what Jake looks like now."

That evening in the back room of the drug store, Bill, Garibaldi, and the mayor of Dodge City discussed matters. The mayor was obviously nervous, as well he might be. But Bill talked about the weather, the way the railroads were spreading across the West, and the chances of another Indian uprising.

Now and then the mayor-druggist was called to the front part of the store to wait on customers. Then, at about nine o'clock, the three men in the back room heard loud talk in the street.

A moment later the store door opened. In stalked a large, tall man wearing, among other things, a frock coat, black Stetson hat, a purple shirt with four enormous diamond studs in its front, and a fancy vest.

On the big fellow's heels came an even dozen men. None of them looked like honest cow hands, or even like common citizens.

"Hey, your honor," shouted the leader, who was Jake Jones. An instant later, he picked up a paper-weight from the top of a counter and crashed it through a glass showcase.

"Hey, your honor!" Jones repeated.

The mayor, alone, came out of the back room.

"Oh, there you are," Jake shouted. "We boys just called in to advise you we are not in favor of closing the saloons of Dodge City at midnight."

With that, the gangster drew off and knocked a row of medicine bottles from the counter. As they crashed on the floor, another figure suddenly emerged from the back room.

It was Hickok. He stood there beside the mayor a moment, then took a couple of steps toward Jake Jones.

"This surely is a surprise," said Wild Bill most

genially. "It's a great pleasure to meet Jake Jones in Dodge City."

The big man in the frock coat stared at the tall man with the long yellow hair. Bill eyed him steadily, an amused smile on his face. But Jake seemed stricken dumb. His mouth was open, yet nothing came out.

"Jake," continued Wild Bill, "don't you figure it's a little crowded in here?"

Without a word, Jake, the king of Dodge City gangsters, turned and went out the door, followed by his crew of thugs.

Wild Bill went to the door and stepped outside. "Oh, Jake," he called. "Just a minute. Better leave ten dollars for the breakage here."

Jake took a gold piece from his pocket and tossed it toward Bill, who doffed his hat and caught it. "Thanks," he said.

Then Wild Bill pulled out the big silver watch he carried. "Jake," he said, "you can get a train out of here at eleven-fifty tonight. Make sure you and these boys of yours are on it—all of you."

Bill reentered the store and gave the money to the mayor.

"Jake won't miss the train," Bill assured him. He was right, too. Jake Jones was never seen again in Dodge City, a fact that tells more than whole pages of the fear and respect which Wild Bill Hickok inspired in the criminals of the frontier.

But neither the mayor of Dodge City nor Garibaldi Smith could prevail on Hickok to serve as city marshal. "I've had enough of it for a while," he said. "I'm going back to Abilene now for a day or two. Then I'll pack my grip and make a trip to my old home in Illinois. Going to make a good visit there."

That is what Wild Bill thought. He didn't know he was about to hear from his old friend Buffalo Bill Cody.

SCOUTS of the PLAINS

BUFFALO BILL
W.F. Cody.

NOW PLAYING NIBLO'S GARDEN.

13: Show Business

AT ABOUT THE TIME WILD BILL WAS GET-
ting ready for his trip to his old home in Illinois,
a journalist and all-around adventurer named
Ned Buntline was in New York City. He was
preparing to stage a play featuring William F.
Cody, better known as Buffalo Bill.

Buntline was famous for his stories for boys

published in dime novels, which were the comic books of the era. On a trip to the great plains, he had met Buffalo Bill, and found him a sensational character who seemed to have the makings of a great showman.

So now Buntline was writing a play, "The Scouts of the Plains."

"Ned," Buffalo Bill told him, "I hear that my old friend Wild Bill has resigned as marshal of Abilene."

"Yes?"

"We ought to have him in our show," said Buffalo Bill.

"Can he act?" Buntline asked.

"Probably not. But he would be a great drawing card."

"He sure would," Ned Buntline agreed. "But isn't he a pretty dangerous character?"

"Not at all. Wild Bill is dangerous only to the kind of people who ought to be in jail anyway."

"He's killed lots of men," Buntline recalled.

"Listen, Ned," Buffalo Bill insisted. "Wild

Bill Hickok never killed a man except in war, or in self-defense."

"Hmmmm." Buntline was thoughtful.

"I know what I'm talking about," Cody insisted. "Wild Bill is the man who is making the frontier towns safe. You should have seen Hays City before he cleaned up the underworld there. You ought to have been in Abilene before Marshal Hickok was appointed."

"Yes, I know he's got a big reputation," said Buntline.

"He's earned it, too. Even people here in the East have read about Wild Bill."

"Well, go ahead and get him if you can. I'll write a part in the show for him."

That was how Wild Bill, packing his grip in Abilene, happened to get a telegram from his old friend in New York:

NEED YOU IN SHOW. GOOD SALARY. LETTER FOLLOWS. BUFFALO BILL CODY.

On arrival of the telegram, Wild Bill decided

to wait for the letter. It came, and with it Buffalo Bill inclosed money for railroad fare to New York. He also made show business sound quite attractive. Knowing, too, that Wild Bill had never been in New York, he gave him some advice.

"When you get to New York," Buffalo Bill wrote, "take a cab from the depot to the Brevoort Hotel, where I am staying. I warn you that New York cab drivers are regular hold-up men. Pay your cab man two dollars and not a cent more."

A week later, in Grand Central station in New York City, people turned their heads to see something new and strange. Down from the cars stepped a tall, lithe, handsome man whose yellow hair fell down over his shoulders. His dress, too, was something. Wild Bill had really togged himself out for his first visit to the big city. He wore a cutaway coat, which bulged slightly on the left hip where a holster hung. He had on a fancy vest. He was wearing his favorite kind of shirt, white and ruffled, a black string tie, high-heeled boots, and a Stetson hat.

Wild Bill did just as Cody had advised. He got into a cab and told the driver to take him to the Hotel Brevoort.

As the Brevoort's doorman let Bill out of the cab, the scout took two dollars from his pocket and proffered the money to the driver.

The surly driver eyed the money, then Hickok. "It's five dollars," he said.

"Two dollars is what you get," Wild Bill said.

"My charge is five dollars."

"You get two dollars," Wild Bill insisted.

"I'll take the rest out of your hide," said the poor, witless cab driver. He came down from his box, took off his coat, and made a pass at the long-haired stranger.

An instant later the driver was rolling in the gutter under the feet of his horse. A policeman came up.

"What goes on here?" asked the bluecoat.

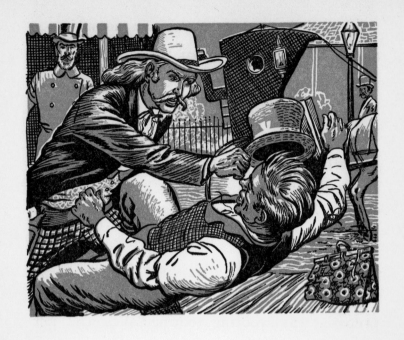

"This robber," replied Hickok softly, "this robber said I owed him five dollars."

"For what?"

"Driving me here from the steam-car depot."

"That's too much," said the policeman. "One dollar would be about right."

"Here's his dollar," and Wild Bill tossed a silver cartwheel at the driver. The policeman and bystanders laughed. Wild Bill went into the hotel lobby.

The hotel manager had seen the affair with

the cab-man. He knew that Buffalo Bill was expecting a man from the West. Before Hickok had got to the lobby, the manager sent a bell-boy to Cody's room with a message. "Mr. Cody," the bellboy was instructed to say, "I think the gentleman you are expecting has arrived."

That was the way Wild Bill Hickok came to New York.

The show Ned Buntline and Buffalo Bill had prepared was a rooting, tooting "Western," perhaps the first of its kind. The characters included Indians, two-gun plainsmen, several mean villains and, of course, a pretty girl named Ella. Ella was to be captured by the redskins and, naturally, rescued in the nick of time by Buffalo Bill and Wild Bill.

The script called for a great deal of gun-play. Bows and arrows were not used. They didn't make any noise. Besides, you could not shoot blank arrows the way you could shoot blank cartridges.

Billboards all over New York City displayed
stirring scenes from "The Scouts of the Plains,"
and the show opened to big business.

Buffalo Bill Cody was a natural actor, a good
one. Wild Bill Hickok was one of the worst ac-
tors ever to set foot on a stage. He thought the
whole thing downright foolish. He couldn't
learn his lines. Or wouldn't, anyway. He and
Cody were always bickering about scenes.

But Wild Bill was a great attraction as a
name, for he was then much better known than
Buffalo Bill. Many people came merely to see
the famous peace officer.

The life wore hard on Wild Bill. Without saying anything more about it, he made up his
mind he didn't want to be an actor. As evidence
of this, he started carrying on in a manner that
would make the rest of the troupe glad to see
him leave the show.

In one of the scenes, Wild Bill raided an Indian camp single-handed, killed or drove off all

the redskins, and rescued the beautiful heroine, Ella. This made a big hit with the audiences. It had been going fairly well for several weeks. Then one day Tall Oak, leader of the Indians, came to Buffalo Bill with a complaint.

"We going away," he said.

"What's the matter? Aren't we paying you enough?"

"Sure," Tall Oak replied. "Pay good. Wild Bill no good."

"Why? What's he doing?"

"He shoot too close to my men. Burn skins."

"So that's it," said Buffalo Bill. "I'll tell Bill to be more careful."

"No good tell him. I tell him. Do no good. Shoot close."

"Leave it to me," Buffalo Bill said.

But when Cody asked Hickok about it, and suggested he be more careful with his blank cartridges, Wild Bill protested that he *was* careful. He said that the Indians were a no-good, belly-aching lot anyway. If they were any good, they wouldn't be in a show.

Nor did the scene improve very much. Wild Bill continued to shoot close to the bare legs and arms of the poor redskins.

But worse than that was coming.

At the end of the big scene, where Hickok rescued Ella from the savages, Wild Bill had to clasp her in his arms. She was to weep with joy and tell Bill what a wonderful hero he was. At this point, the man high in the gallery turned the big spotlight on Bill and the maiden.

One night Wild Bill clasped Ella, as he was supposed to do. Down beat the white glare of the powerful spotlight. Then—without a word Wild Bill drew a gun and shot the lamp to splinters!

When the thick glass of the lamp crashed, then tinkled down over the startled audience, Buffalo Bill knew that Hickok's gun had been loaded with more than just powder. So did the spotlight operator.

Wild Bill drew a gun and shot the lamp to splinters!

And, as Wild Bill was heard to remark, "That was one way of getting out of show business." He packed his suitcase and got aboard a train for the West.

14: The Black Hills

IN CHICAGO, WHERE HE STOPPED A COUPLE of days, Wild Bill received challenging news. Friends of Phil Coe, the gambler whom Hickok had shot and killed in Abilene, were planning to gang up on Hickok when he returned from the East. They had sworn revenge. They would kill him the moment he stepped from the train, no matter in what town.

Wild Bill sent a telegram to a newspaper friend in Cheyenne, Wyoming, asking him to print the news that Wild Bill Hickok was returning from the East. He would arrive in Cheyenne at such and such an hour on such and such a day on the Union Pacific train.

The Cheyenne paper promptly printed the item. The whole town grew more excited by the hour, thinking there would be some wonderful gun-play when the train arrived.

Crowds began to congregate around the Cheyenne depot a full hour before the train was due from Chicago. The train was on time. As it rolled into the station, the crowd saw a lone figure standing on the rear platform of the last passenger coach. It was Wild Bill, all right. He stood there casually, hands at his sides, ready for whatever might happen.

But Coe's friends never showed up. Instead Bill's arrival set off the greatest ovation Cheyenne had ever seen. Two thousand people cheered wildly as Bill doffed his hat, bowed, and stepped down to the platform. There he was all but mobbed by men who knew and admired a brave man when they saw one.

Wild Bill was bundled into an open carriage and driven up the main street with the mayor beside him. Following them were several hundred people, many of them mounted cow hands.

A bit later Wild Bill surprised almost everybody by getting married. The bride was a widow, Mrs. Agnes Lake, who had been in show business. She was a tight-rope performer who had also trained lions. She had toured the British Isles and Europe, and at one time had her own show.

The couple went first to Cincinnati, then to St. Louis, where they rented a house and probably thought they were settling down in the usual manner of married people.

The Hickoks got along together very well, and seemed happy enough, but Bill began to find things rather tame. For twenty years he had lived a dangerous life. He liked it that way. He liked excitement. He enjoyed the companionship of men, and the free and easy ways of the frontier.

It was now the spring of 1876. The snow of the plains had gone. The country was warm again. Wild flowers grew riotously everywhere. Even lazy men grew restless. And then came news of a gold strike, a tremendous gold strike, the biggest the United States had known since Forty-Nine.

This time the land of treasure was the Black Hills region of Dakota Territory. The newspapers of St. Louis, where Wild Bill was trying to live the life of a contented married man, were filled with stories of fortunes being made almost overnight. Men were on the move. All of the frontier towns and cities felt the surge toward the Black Hills.

This was dangerous Indian country. The tribes of the Black Hills sent a chief to tell the

Great White Father in Washington that they would resist the coming of pale-faces. And the pale-faces, of course, paid no heed.

In St. Louis a company of two hundred men was forming to make a rush for the new gold fields. They sent a spokesman to ask Wild Bill Hickok to act as their guide. Bill was ready; here was a good excuse to return to the way of life he liked. He told the agent he would guide their company so long as he was also in command of the group.

"The Black Hills are perhaps the most dangerous section of the United States right now," Bill said. "I am willing to go, and I am sure I can get you to the diggings safely, so long as I run the whole shebang. There must be discipline."

The spokesman was glad to agree. He added that the company would pay Bill one thousand dollars to land them in Deadwood Gulch, which was said to be the richest diggings of the strike.

Wild Bill got into his working clothes,

strapped on his guns, and said good-bye to his wife. The company left by train for Cheyenne, where it was joined by another fifty men.

Meanwhile, Wild Bill was seeking information as to which was the better of two routes into the Black Hills. One was by Bismarck, in Northern Dakota Territory; the other was directly overland from Cheyenne. Bill chose the latter as the quicker route. It might not be quite so safe as the other, but Bill figured that with discipline—no drinking on the trail was one of his rules—the danger of Indian attack could be forestalled.

With iron rule and great skill, Wild Bill led his company of two hundred and fifty men overland and into the Black Hills, and so to the roaring new town of Deadwood City, set fair in the gulch which men gone mad were staking from one end to the other for their claims.

Bill was promptly paid his fee. Without losing a minute, he struck out alone to return to Cheyenne, riding at night, hiding out by day. The trip was made without incident, although many parties of gold seekers were being attacked by Indians.

Back in Cheyenne, Wild Bill looked up an old friend, Charles Utter, better known as Colorado Charley.

"Charley," said Bill, "do you want to try your luck with me as a gold miner?"

"Yes, sir, Bill, I do. Always wanted to try my hand with a pan and shovel."

"Well, I've been to Deadwood," Wild Bill told his friend. "The whole country around there is filling up with men who want to be gold miners."

"Finding gold is pretty much luck, ain't it?" Charley wanted to know.

"Yes, mostly luck," Bill agreed. "You and I don't know anything about mining, but we'll have just as good a chance of hitting it rich as any of the guys who think they are experts."

"If you hit it big, you're an expert. Ain't that it?"

"That's the way it is," said Bill. "Go buy your-self a pick, a shovel, and a pan. Yes, and a little grub. We can leave any old time."

"I'll be ready in the morning," Charley prom-ised. "I got a good hoss."

Before daylight next morning, the two would-be miners rode out of Cheyenne. They followed Wild Bill's practice on the previous trip; they rode at night. In daylight they holed up near water in the willows and cottonwoods. The near-est they came to seeing an Indian was when they found a spot where a band had camped for the night.

Arrived at Deadwood, Charley and Bill found a place as lawless as Hays City or Abilene had been before Marshal Hickok had worked his wonders on those two towns. It seemed as if all the thieves, crooked gamblers, and assorted cut-throats of the frontier had flocked to this raw new settlement in Deadwood Gulch. Wild Bill recognized more than two hundred criminals in the place.

Up and down the gulch little saloons stood side by side, here and there broken by a dance hall. Gambling rooms ran twenty-four hours a day, with the dealers working twelve-hour shifts.

Charley and Bill slipped into town as quietly as possible, and set out staking a claim apiece. Wild Bill was here as a miner, and he didn't want the job of town marshal. But his fame had come with him. Within two days, every thief and bully in Deadwood knew the famous frontier peace-officer was in town. So did every decent miner. A group of the latter sent a man to ask Wild Bill if he would act as marshal.

"No," replied Bill, "I am here like you fellers to work a claim. I'm a miner. You get somebody else."

Charley and Bill went to work. They cut trees and put up a small cabin beside a small stream about half a mile from Deadwood City. With this place as headquarters, the two men worked around in the hills, seeking what miners call "indications" of gold—signs that gold was present.

Charley Utter told afterward that his partner seemed to have a feeling of impending trouble. One day while the two men rested and looked down the gulch, Bill suddenly spoke up. "Charley, I have a hunch that I'm in my last camp and will never leave this gulch alive."

"Quit your dreaming," Charley said.

"I'm not dreaming, Charley. Something tells me my time is up."

"What you need is something for your liver."

"No, Charley, it isn't my liver," Bill insisted. "I just know I'm not far from the end of the trail."

Colorado Charley tried to make light of it by laughing, and he began to tease Bill about having silly notions. Bill laughed, too, but his laughter did not sound wholehearted to Charley.

Wild Bill knew, of course, that the crooked element of Deadwood both feared and hated him. Among the toughs was more than one man who had once had to leave Hays City or Abilene because of Wild Bill. Two of these were Tim Brady and Johnny Varnes, who considered themselves the boss gangsters of the camp. Now in their Deadwood shacks they discussed Hickok, and agreed it would take a brave man to kill him.

15: . . . . *with His Boots On*

DEADWOOD'S TWO LEADING MOBSTERS, TIM Brady and Johnny Varnes, naturally wanted to rid the town of Hickok, fearing he might change his mind and accept the proffered job of peace-officer. Neither mobster, however, was eager for a fight with Hickok. They knew too well his lightning speed with a gun, and the skill with which he used it.

"Why not use Broken-Nose-Jack to get rid of Hickok?" was the thought that came to both the gang leaders.

Broken-Nose-Jack McCall was one of the boomtown crooks at Deadwood. His nose had been bashed in when somebody struck it hard with a gun butt.

McCall was a weak man whose chief ambition was to get enough money to buy the whiskey he thought he needed. He drank a lot of whiskey. To earn the necessary cash he picked the pockets of drunken miners, and worked as janitor in Deadwood saloons and dance halls. Perhaps, thought Varnes and Brady, they could get him to shoot Wild Bill. They kept Broken-Nose-Jack supplied with free whiskey. They pretended to admire his ability as a tough hombre. They told him he could become the hero of Deadwood if he shot Wild Bill.

Again and again Brady and Varnes kept drill-

ing away at one idea: The man who killed Wild
Bill Hickok would automatically become the
most famous man, not only in Deadwood, but
in the whole West.

It wasn't easy to persuade McCall that he was
the right man. Twice, Brady and Varnes thought
they had convinced him. And twice McCall had
failed them. "It ain't the right time," he had
said.

Rumors grew that Wild Bill would soon put
on a star and become city marshal of Deadwood.
The story was heard in every saloon. Honest
men told one another that the local murders
and nightly robberies would soon cease. Wild
Bill would put a stop to lawlessness.

Now came the second of August. It was a blis-
tering hot day. The sun beat down into the
gulch that held Deadwood City. Not a breath of
air stirred. Even the leaves of the aspens and
the cottonwoods were still. No bird sang. The
gold-crazed miners had ceased work. They lay
under their tents or in their cabins, or they

went to play cards and drink liquor in the saloons of Deadwood.

At noon that day, Tim Brady and Johnny Varnes called Broken-Nose-Jack McCall into the back room of the IXL saloon.

"Listen," Brady said, after he had set out a bottle to which McCall helped himself. "Listen, are you ready to make your mark?"

"You mean—you mean, Wild Bill?"

"Of course," Brady snapped. "He's in the Bella Union right now, playing poker. He's relaxed. He's enjoying himself. He ain't thinking of trouble. He don't know you are a real gunman."

"But he's powerful quick," McCall protested.

"Always somebody quicker. Johnny Varnes and me think McCall is quicker than Bill Hickok. Have another drink."

Broken-Nose McCall accepted the offer.

"What's more, Jack," Brady went on, "by wiping out Hickok you sure will be the biggest hero between Chicago and the Pacific coast."

"Yeah, but . . ."

"Tell you what, Jack, my boy. Me and Johnny here figure we can pay you a hundred dollars, good gold dust, if you'll take care of that guy."

"A hundred dollars?" McCall's bleary eyes lighted as he reached again for the bottle. "A hundred dollars cash?"

"Yes, sir, cash. Twenty-five down. The rest after you've done the work."

Tim Brady hauled a chamois-skin poke from his pocket. He opened the end and let the glittering stuff trickle out onto the table, where it seemed to dance in the light. McCall looked at it, fascinated.

"Twenty-five now," repeated Brady, "and seventy-five more as soon as you come back from the Bella Union."

McCall suddenly reached for the bottle again. He poured and drank. He stuck out his chest. "Gimme the twenty-five," he said. "I'm on my way."

Brady brought scales from the barroom. He

put a small weight in one scale, then sifted dust into the other until the two balanced.

"Here you are. Here's a generous twenty-five dollars."

McCall put the stuff into a tobacco box which he stuffed into his pocket.

He pulled out his gun. He looked to see that all the chambers were loaded, then returned the weapon to its holster.

"I'll be seeing you in a few minutes," he said, and swaggered out of the IXL. He started up Main Street. Fifty yards away stood the Bella Union saloon. In that saloon was Bill Hickok.

The sun beat down hotter than ever. In swarming Deadwood there was scarcely a man moving on the street as Jack McCall set forth on his errand of murder.

He moved ahead slowly now, doggedly, almost automatically, as though he were some sort of mechanical man set in motion.

In the Bella Union a dozen men lounged along the bar, drinking casually. Of the six gambling tables only one was in use. At this table a game of poker was in progress. In it were Charley Rich, Carl Mann, a former Mississippi River pilot named Captain Massey, and Wild Bill Hickok.

For some reason never explained, Wild Bill sat with his back to the saloon entrance.

So far as is known, Hickok had never before sat thus in a public place. He knew he was a marked man wherever he was. He knew there were hundreds of dangerous men who might chance a shot at him if his back were turned. He knew there were criminals in Deadwood ready to kill him.

Yet here he was, Bill Hickok, the alert and watchful, cards in his hands, his back to the door.

On the wall behind the long bar was a clock. And now, above the hum of talk in the Bella Union, it struck three times.

Just then Jack McCall came in the door. He was a nobody, and nobody paid him any attention. He went to the bar.

"Gimme a whiskey," said McCall. The bartender set out a bottle and glass. McCall poured a drink, paid for it, then drank.

The poker game continued, accompanied by the usual small talk of the players.

Unnoticed by the players and unheeded by others in the room, McCall moved toward the poker table. For a brief moment he stood there, motionless. Then, before anybody quite took in what was going on, McCall drew his gun, stepped close behind Hickok's chair and fired.

McCall's gun was less than three feet from the back of Hickok's head. He couldn't miss.

Wild Bill shuddered, then slumped forward across the table. He never spoke. He was dead. His body slid from the chair to the floor. His left hand still held five cards—aces and eights.

The bullet had passed through Hickok's head, then plowed into the forearm of Captain Massey.

The other players leaped to their feet. McCall covered them with his smoking gun.

McCall drew his gun, stepped close behind Hickok . . .

"Lay off me. Lay off. All of you," he cried, as he backed toward the door. Once outside, he turned and ran, but not far. He was rattled, frightened, this would-be gunman, and in his great fear he dodged into a butcher shop. And there he was arrested almost immediately by Sheriff Isaac Brown, assisted, it is sometimes said, by a woman known as Calamity Jane.

Jack McCall made no attempt to escape ar- rest. Many bystanders said McCall had been promised he would not be prosecuted, and that was why he made no attempt to run away.

Funeral services were held next day at the cabin where Charley Utter was now to live alone; and Wild Bill was buried after a clergy- man spoke briefly.

Thus passed James Butler Hickok, the Wild Bill of the plains, the man who more than any other had brought civilized order to the fron- tier. It was ironic that he should have died from the violence he himself had done so much to subdue. It was strange, too, that the drunken coward who killed him was possibly the least worthy of any of Wild Bill's many enemies.

Bill Hickok was not quite forty years old when he died. How many times in those thirty-nine years he had been close to death, not even he could have told. Surely, there had been many such times, and then—he had sat once, only once, with his back to a door. . . .

At the trial of McCall, he was found not guilty by what many believed to have been a "packed" jury; that is, one carefully selected by underworld interests in Deadwood. McCall left Deadwood at once.

But that was not the end of Broken-Nose McCall.

Not content with going free of the murder of Wild Bill, Jack McCall arrived in Custer City with the hundred dollars in blood money. He proceeded to get drunk. He bragged that he had deliberately set out to kill Hickok. He sneered that the "evidence" on which he had been freed was perjured, made up of lies.

Colonel May of Deadwood, who had prosecuted McCall at the trial, heard about the boasts McCall was making. He swore out a warrant for the assassin's arrest.

McCall was taken in Custer City, then transported to Yankton, capital of Dakota Territory. There he was tried for murder. A jury found him guilty in the first degree.

On March 1, 1877, Broken-Nose-Jack McCall was taken from his cell and hanged. The fame he had hoped would be his as the greatest gunman of the West did not survive his burial.

Most Americans today have heard of Wild Bill Hickok. Not one in a hundred thousand or more ever heard of Jack McCall.

In history, Wild Bill is a controversial figure. Some men praise him. Others are critical of him. But no man ever expressed doubt as to his courage, his cold nerve, his skill with any sort of gun.

Wild Bill's memory is cherished today in Deadwood where, in Mount Moriah cemetery, there is a monument erected to his memory by his old partner, Colorado Charley Utter. No visitor fails to see it. Because of souvenir hunters, the monument is now protected by a network of steel wire.

Wild Bill probably died at the right time. By 1876 railroads and schools and churches and farms and courts and, yes, police departments, had spread to nearly all parts of the West. Civilization had come. The bad old West was fading. It had almost disappeared. No single man played a greater part in the change than James Butler Hickok—Marshal Wild Bill.

Bibliography

Connelley, William E., *Wild Bill and His Era,*
   1933.

Wilstach, Frank J., *Wild Bill Hickok,* 1926.

Custer, G. A., *Wild Life on the Plains,* 1874.

Custer, E. B., *Tenting on the Plains,* 1887.

Harris, Frank, *My Life and Loves,* Vol. 1, 1923.

Eisele, W. E., *The Real Wild Bill Hickok,* 1931.

Holbrook, Stewart H., *Little Annie Oakley and
   Other Rugged People,* 1948.